GATHERING THE TIDE

GATHERING THE TIDE

An Anthology of
Contemporary Arabian Gulf Poetry

EDITED BY
PATTY PAINE, JEFF LODGE,
AND SAMIA TOUATI

GATHERING THE TIDE
An Anthology of Contemporary Arabian Gulf Poetry

Published by
Ithaca Press
8 Southern Court
South Street
Reading
RG1 4QS
UK

www.ithacapress.co.uk
www.twitter.com/Garnetpub
www.facebook.com/Garnetpub
thelevant.wordpress.com

Ithaca Press is an imprint of Garnet Publishing Ltd.

First Edition 2011

ISBN-13: 978-0-86372-375-9

British Library Cataloguing-in-Publication Data
A catalogue record for this book is available from the British Library

Jacket design by Garnet Publishing
Cover illustration by Nawar Al-Mutlaq, Aisha Al-Naama,
Al Hussein Wanas and Ameera Makki
Typeset by Samantha Barden

Printed in Lebanon by International Press
interpress@int-press.com

CONTENTS

꩜

Preface xv

Acknowledgements xix

One Poet's Story xix
Nimah Ismail Nawwab

"Because the Sand Was Made for Me Alone to Splash My Ink There":
New Poetry from the Gulf xxvii
David Wojahn

꩜

POETS FROM BAHRAIN 1
Qassim Haddad 2
Poets 2
Stone 4
The Friends There 6
Body 8
A Prayer for Travel 9
The Café's Memory 10
Words from a Young Night 11

Fawzia Al Sindi 16
Awakening 16
From *Less Than Ink* 20

Ali Al Sharqawi 23
From *Psalm 23: To the Singer's Nectar* 23
Beyond Language 31

Hameed Al Qaed 32
Obsession 32

v

Painting 34
Verses 35

Ahmed ALajmi 37
Morning in Paris 37
Enjoyment 39

Laala Kashef Alghata 40
Regard Me Sadly 40
Roadside Flowers 42

Ali Abdulla Khalifa 43
The Clover Flower 43
In the Presence of the One I Love 45
No One 46
A Window for Longing 48

Hamda Khamis 49
Poems from the Collection *The Bliss of Love* 49
Couple 56
Ray 56
Those Not for Me 57
Without Reason 59

Ali Al Jallawi 60
According to a Cloud Whispering to her Sister 60
You . . . 62
Trying to Understand 63
The Wisdom of Hallaj 64

Karim Radhi 65
Chief of Staff 65
Missile 65
Nights of War 66
Pretext 66
Soldier 67
War Martyr 67
War Poet 67
War Reporter 68
War Traders 68

Adel Khozam 69
White Shame 69
Do This 71
Sliding 72
Destiny 72
Transient Love 73
The Heroism of a Thread 74
Strange Circles 75

⸎

POETS FROM KUWAIT 79
Souad Al-Mubarak Al-Sabah 80
A Woman from Kuwait 80
Female 2000 84
Ingratitude 86
Love Poem 1 87
My Body is a Palm Tree that Grows on Bahr al-Arab 91

Ghanima Zaid Al Harb 96
Escaping from the Coma Cage 96
The Sparkle 98

Haifa Al Sanousi 99
It is not Fair 99
Birth of Words 101

Khalifa Al Woqayyan 102
The Harvest 102
A Pulse 104
An Elegy 105

Mohammad Almoghrabi 108
The Mural of Arrogance 108

Saadia Mufarreh 110
Refrigerator 110
Loss 111

vii

Soon She Will Leave 112
Distance 114

Salem Sayar Mohsin Al Anzi 115
The Storm 115
Bundle of Wounds 118
A Miserable Childhood 119

Shurooq Amin 121
Another Day of *Eid* 121
Fate of the Gulf Mariner 123
Olfactory Bazaar 125

∾

POETS FROM OMAN 127
Saif Al Rahbi 128
Distant Waters 128
Arrival 129
Bells will not Toll Tonight 129
Friends 130
Museum of Shadows 131
No Country We Headed To 132
Our Old House 133
Scream 134
Suitcase 135
A Tramp Dreaming of Nothing 136
Under the Roofs of Morning 139
Water Blessed by Prophets 140

Abudullah al Ryami 141
Please Don't Give Birth! 141
Speed 143

Ghalya Al Said 144
The Car 144
Malika and the Zar Dance 145

Mohamed al-Harthy 147
A Little Before Reaching Death 147
Apology to the Dawn 148
Pawns of Sand 149
At a Slant Angle 151

Reem Al Lawati 153
The Chronology of Water 153
May Love Be Praised 155
The Psalms of Loneliness 157

Zahir al-Ghafri 159
The Angel of Power 159
A Room at the End of the World 160
Those Years 161

POETS FROM QATAR 163
Soad Al Kuwari 164
The Flood 164
Modernity in the Desert 167
The Queen of the Mountains 168

Maryam Ahmad Al-Subaiey 171
The Invisible Army 171

Dhabiya Khamis 173
Delhi's Gardens 173
The History of that Tree 175
Scented Walls 177
Sky Rain 179

Zakiyya Malallah 180
Little Tales 180
If You Were Mine 184
Blending 185
Observance 186
Isolation 186

Abdullah Al Salem 187
A Celebration of Loss 187
Downtrodden People 189
Emergency Meeting 192

ℭ

POETS FROM SAUDI ARABIA 195
Nimah Ismail Nawwab 196
The Streets of Makkah 196
The Longing 198
Banishment 199
Arabian Nights 202
The Ambush 204
Illusions and Realities 206
Freedom Writers 208

Ali Gharam Allah Al Domaini 209
The Signs 209
I Am Fatima 214
A Kiss 218
A Moon 218

Ashjan Al Hendi 219
Butterflies 219
A Couple 220
Gray Hair 222
I Swear by the God of *Al-Kawthar* 223
In Search of the Other 225
It Has Ears 226
Moon Wars 227

Abir Zaki 231
And You Call Me a Feminist . . . ! 231
But she is never a loser . . . 233

Fowziyah Abu-Khalid 235
My Late Hours with Me 235
Craving 237

Acidity Smell 238
Pregnancy Smell 239
Ripe Date Smell 239
Labor Smell 240
Fenugreek Smell 240
Anise Smell 241
Baby Smell 241
Tuful: Noonday Rainbow 242
Two Little Girls 243
Numerical Conjecture 245

Abdallah Al Saikhan **248**
Star of Ink 248
The Poet 250
Sword 250
Maliha 251

Thuraya Al Arrayed **252**
Desert Dreams 252
The Doors; The Game of Times 255
Moments of Silence 259
The Stillborn 261

Ghazi Al Ghosaibi **263**
Dusting the Color from Roses 263
In the Old Street 266
Oh, Desert 268
Which One of Us Returned Safely? 270

∽

POETS FROM THE UNITED ARAB EMIRATES 275
Nujoom Alghanem **276**
Blazing Fires 276
Immigrant 278
The Darkness is Thick 279
Monks 279
I Remember Him 280
By the Seashore 280

xi

Distance 281
Seaflower 282
The Snow of Mounts 283
Loyalty 284

Shihab Ghanem 285
Bakhbookh 285
Behind the Iron Curtain 287
Entrapped 289
Illuminations in a Valley without Vegetation 290
Radiance 293

His Highness Sheikh Mohammed bin Rashid Al Maktoum 295
I Pictured the Dreams – Rashid and Hamdan 295
Poem of Condolence 297
Swords of Beauty 299

Ahmed Rashid Thani 301
On the Table 301
Valleys 303

Khulood Al Mu'alla 304
Body's Winter 304
An Unexceptional Poet 305
The Language of the Sea 307
Incessant Pain 307
Egg 307

Amal Khalid Sultan Al Qassemi 308
Four Leaves of Basil 308

Anwar Alkhatib 312
No Land for Passersby 312
Two Gates to Redemption 314
When We Grow Older 317

Maisoon Saqr Al Qasimi 319
A Mad Man Who does not Love Me 319
How Lucky the Fisherman Is 333

I Am the Only Cat Here 334
Instead of Mirrors 335

Thani Al-Suwaidi 336
A Day 336
Delusion 338
The Shepherd 339
Testament 340
Transience 341
Poems for the Wind 344

Khalid Albudoor 346
Everything 346
Lantern 347
Soon 348
All That We Have 349

⌒℘⌒

The Translators 353
The Editors 361
Credits 363

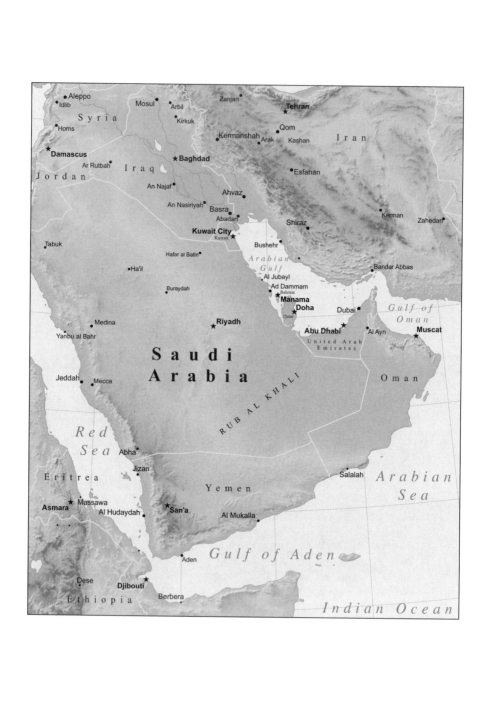

PREFACE

It started simply enough. In an introduction to poetry class, after reading the required books list, the students wanted to know why the list did not include an anthology of contemporary poetry from the GCC (Gulf Cooperation Council) countries of the Gulf region.

Why not indeed?

After all, this was a poetry class not in the US but at Virginia Commonwealth University in Doha, Qatar (VCUQatar), where the majority of students are from Qatar and the Gulf region. VCUQatar offers degrees in painting and printmaking, and in graphic, fashion, and interior design. It shares a sprawling thirty-five-hundred-acre campus with five other universities that together form Education City, the largest gathering of American universities outside the US. Education City is a venture of the Qatar Foundation, a private, chartered, non-profit organization founded in 1995 by decree of His Highness Sheikh Hamad bin Khalifa Al Thani, Emir of Qatar. The Qatar Foundation focuses on fostering education, scientific research, and community development.

Around the same time as that simple, but important, question was asked, the Qatar Foundation issued a call for Undergraduate Research Experience Program (UREP) grants. The intent of the UREP grant is to "engage undergraduates under the mentorship of faculty members in all universities in Qatar on research projects related to Qatar's national needs." The students expressed a clear need: the creation of an anthology of poetry written by the poets closest to them. We were awarded a grant to work with students to collect and translate poems from established and emerging poets in the region for use in future poetry classes.

This anthology would not exist without the four students who worked with us on this project: Aisha Khalid Al-Naama, Fatima Abdulhameed Mostafawi, Hend Mubarak Aleidan, and Sara Marwan Al-Qatami. We spent countless hours together identifying poets in the region who merited inclusion in an anthology. We moved through poems, sometimes word by word, to translate them from Arabic into English. We attended conferences on translation together, and we formed our own translation workshops with poets and translators who were kind enough to come to Doha to work with us. Our students' work is present in every aspect of this anthology, but we are especially delighted and proud that poems they have translated appear within. It is particularly impressive when one remembers that VCUQatar is a school of design and that the time and effort Aisha, Hend, Sara, and Fatima dedicated to this project was outside their course work.

We made an unlikely trio of editors of an anthology of Arabic poetry in translation. Patty and Jeff have editing and publishing experience in poetry and fiction, but none of us were expert in Middle Eastern poetry, and only Samia, originally from Morocco, is fluent in Arabic. What we did have, though, were those four eager and outstanding students, support both from VCUQatar and the Qatar Foundation, and our own passion for the project driven by a desire to give voice to the poets of this region who have been largely neglected by western readers and to give something back to Qatar, a country that generously welcomed us and entrusted us to educate its young people.

The Gulf region has a wealth of talented poets, and in the early stages of compiling our anthology *Banipal*, *www.jehat.com*, and the anthologies *The Poetry of Arab Women*, edited by Nathalie Handal, *Modern Arabic Poetry*, edited by Salma Khadra Jayyusi, and *A Crack in the Wall*, edited by Margaret Obank and Samuel Shimon, were essential resources for identifying them. (A more complete list of the people and resources we owe a debt of gratitude to follows.) We expected this project to be challenging, but finding contact information for the poets we hoped to include in the anthology was an unexpected difficulty. Had we been looking for American poets, the process would have been as simple as searching Facebook, or a university faculty page. Our Gulf poets were much harder to find. There is a higher degree of privacy in the Middle East, and of the poets represented in the anthology only a very small number are career poets. Several work at newspapers and magazines, others for TV stations, and several hold government positions, including the Emir of Dubai and the Prime Minster and the Vice President of the United Arab Emirates. Others own businesses or work in the sciences or law. We are grateful to all those, from poets, to translators, to friends of friends, who helped us make contact with poets. Still, there are several poets we would have liked to include in this collection but were unable to find. Their exclusion is regrettable, though not intentional.

We decided early on that we didn't want to merely collect and re-present the relatively small number of poems that had been translated and were available to a western audience. Our goal was to give voice to as many poets and poems from the Gulf region as we could. As daunting and time consuming as it was, we wanted the anthology to contain work translated specifically for this publication. We worked with an incredible team of translators, and we are proud that over seventy percent of this anthology is made up of poems that will appear in print in English for the first time.

We thank our translators for their commitment to honoring the voice and intent of the poets. We worked closely with the translators and poets, and at times translator and poet worked together line by line. Arabic is a rich, and richly nuanced and musical, language. It is difficult to capture in English, but we believe our translators did extra-ordinary work in echoing the voice of the poets. We tried to maintain a light touch as editors, editing primarily to address mechanics and clarity. Translation and editing is painstaking and difficult work. It requires a delicate balance, and a constant struggle between bringing the poem to the reader and the reader to the poem. We tried very hard to maintain this balance and to create translations that are accessible to a western reader but have not been made over into western poems.

Gathering the Tide was over three years in the making, and it is the product of the work of nearly a hundred poets, translators, editors, and others. We hope that it will enable its readers to come to understand and appreciate differences among peoples of different regions and varying cultures even as they gain a greater sense of, and appreciation for, all that unites us. The poets in this anthology grapple with the same hopes and fears as we all do. They celebrate life, they contend with loss. They wonder at contradiction, they marvel at paradox. They do so in a region with a long and exceptional history, and with a fascinating and rapidly evolving present.

We owe our greatest of debts to the stunningly talented poets of this region. We have been amazed by their generosity and overwhelmed by their enthusiasm. They entrusted us with their poems, and we hope we have honored their trust.

Finally, we would like to acknowledge and express gratitude to all who supported this endeavor. Foremost, we thank Allyson Vanstone, Dean of Virginia Commonwealth University in Qatar, who has supported the project fully from inception to completion. Also at VCUQatar, we thank all the faculty and staff who at one time or another have lent their support and encouragement, especially Bill McGee, Peter Chomowicz, Charles Bleick, Noel Knille, Byrad Yyelland, Brian Harris, Lolwa Ibrahim

M Abdulla, Carmina Celeridad, and our colleagues in the English program: Robin Fetherston, Diana Woodcock, Jesse Ulmer, and Lauren Maas.

We thank the four VCUQatar students who contributed the beautiful cover design: Nawar Al-Mutlaq, Aisha Al-Naama, Al Hussein Wanas, and Ameera Makki. We also thank the graphic design professors who supervised them, Muneera Spence and Law Alsobrook.

We offer special thanks to our friend and colleague David Wojahn for his insightful introduction and to his former student Khaled Mattawa for his early participation and advice. We offer special thanks also to Dan Nunn, formerly of Garnet Publishing/Ithaca Press, who was the first publisher to express interest in our proposal and whose enthusiasm and professionalism persuaded us to choose Garnet/Ithaca over other publishers.

And, of course, we thank everyone at Garnet Publishing/Ithaca Press, but especially Arash Hejazi, for his support, insights, and patience.

We thank Dr. Shihab Ghanem for the valuable historical information he provided, and we thank the Ministries of Culture in each of the Gulf states, Dr. Khalid Abdellatif Al Shaiji, the Kuwaiti Writers Guild, and Cat Lucas, campaigns officer of English PEN.

We thank the editors of the several publications who allowed us to reprint poems that they had published previously. A complete list can be found in the Credits section at the end of this anthology.

We thank our family and our friends for their faith in our work and their patience, as we so often gave it priority over them. They are too numerous to mention, but they know who they are.

And we must acknowledge again two pioneers in the dissemination of contemporary Arab literature – including, of course, poetry – to the English-speaking world, both for their contributions to this book and for their contributions to literature as a whole. Since 1998, *Banipal: Magazine of Modern Arab Literature* has published in nearly forty issues hundreds of poets and writers, strengthening the dialogue between cultures and bringing the joy of Arab literature to multitudes. Founded and edited by Margaret Obank and Iraqi author Samuel Shimon, it has set the standard for all of us who follow. Also, poet, playwright, writer, and editor Nathalie Handal, with the *Poetry of Arab Women: a Contemporary Anthology*, published in 2000, and *Language for a New Century: Contemporary Poetry from the Middle East, Asia, and Beyond*, published in 2008, showed us what an excellent anthology should be.

Patty Paine, Jeff Lodge, and Samia Touati

ACKNOWLEDGEMENTS

This publication was made possible in part by a grant from the Qatar National Research Fund under its Undergraduate Research Experience Program. Its contents are solely the responsibility of the authors and do not necessarily represent the official views of the Qatar National Research Fund.

ONE POET'S STORY

Nimah Ismail Nawwab

The work of Gulf poets is deeply rooted in the pre-Islamic oral tradition of sharing wisdom, thoughts, stories, joys, and trials. The long oral history of the Gulf region from the pre-Islamic era accords poets a special place of honor in Arab culture. Poets were the historians and oracles of their tribes – very much the voice of their people. Poets continue to be held in high esteem, and events, both formal and informal, are often initiated with passages of poetry.

The poetry of this region offers a window into a world teeming with creativity. Even for a Saudi Arabian poet originally from Mecca (now known as Makkah), the spiritual heartland of Muslims, discovering the work of Gulf poets is exhilarating. The unique voices of the poets collected here create a tapestry that stirs the heart and soul and offers insight into the rich culture and history of the region.

Gulf poets, like all poets, address universal themes such as love and loss, but they also encompass themes that are uniquely Arab, and uniquely *Khaliji*, or Gulf-related. The identity of those poets is multi-layered and the result is a poetry that is complex, dynamic, and distinctive.

The role of faith in the lives of Gulf poets cannot be separated from our work, as religion forms a major aspect of our identity and voice. Even with evolving spirituality and the rise of liberalism, faith still remains an irrefutable aspect of who we are. Our sense of identity is also influenced by nationalism, political circumstances, and the complexity of life in this volatile region. This region has endured political unrest, and this upheaval is often explored through poetry. Alienation, patriotism, pride, and even tribalism are often expressed as loss, frustration, bitterness, and pessimism in the wake of wars, such as the latest Gulf war. It is interesting to note how some poems are overtly political while the politics in other poems is submerged and relies on metaphor and allusion.

Non-political poems, in general, are a unique combination of romanticism melded with Arab culture and nationalism. These poems take on themes of love, relationships, family, and social life as well as offering praise of certain figures in present or past history. In both political and non-political poems, intense emotions drive poetic expression.

The oil boom and sudden wealth has led to a contemplation of the westernization, the technology, and the rapid development that is taking place in this region. Poets who once composed poems about the desert, hunting, and pearl diving now also write about the challenge of balancing tradition with modernity. Now there are poems about shopping malls, trips abroad, the gender gap, and the job market. Although a great deal has been written about the massive development in the Gulf by journalists and scholars, poets offer a unique, and necessary, perspective. As Aristotle said: "Poetry is finer and more philosophical than history; for poetry expresses the universal, and history only the particular."

Challenges

From afar it is easy to assume that Gulf poets lead lives of ease and are constantly sought out and published. However, the reality is that like poets elsewhere Gulf poets search for sources of inspiration, strive to produce good work, and hope to publish poetry that will withstand the test of time. Arab poets, however, face some challenges that western poets may not.

In middle and high school, most students generally read the classic poets who are part of the required reading in literature classes; however, we are not taught the rudiments of creative writing as a craft. The lack of Master of Fine Arts programs in creative writing at the university level is another impediment in the pursuit of poetic studies in the region as a whole. Literature studies are inclusive of all types of literature, but the study of poetry falls within the study of literature as a whole; it is not a separate discipline. A program to write poetry formally is not offered at any university in the Middle East, unlike journalism, for example. The lack of poetry workshops, conferences, specialized poetry publications, and established networks also creates gaps that need to be filled to help nurture established and emerging voices. There is also a serious lack of mentoring, and this is a major problem because one-on-one attention to craft is very much needed.

Although Arab poets lack established networks, it can be argued that poetry is much more popular in the Middle East than in the west. Popular songs by celebrated male and female singers have for centuries included the verses of renowned poets. In this way the general populace is exposed to the work of master poets and the beauty of the Arabic language. Popular magazines, newspapers, and women's journals often include poetry features by amateur and established poets. Even children's magazines include poems by classic or modern poets.

An extremely popular television show called *Millionaire Poet* has led to a phenomenon where the media and public play a role in assessing a poet's work in a competitive, public arena that includes poetry judging and audience feedback. The pros and cons of the show have become subject of much debate in the region. Some argue that it has led to a rise in pride and tribalism as poets often sing the praises of their local tribes or political figures while seeking to gain fame, fortune, and votes. The caliber of the work is also a note of contention, and this has resulted in debates over classic, spoken, and modern Arabic trends in poetry and the strength of each.

This show has drawn a massive audience and hundreds of competitors, and has created another link in the history of the primacy of poetry in the region. Pre-Islamic poetry competitions at renowned sites such as *Suq Ukaz* drew poets from all parts of the area as they engaged in poetic battles that often included work composed on the spot. This chain in the history of poetry is one that most poets will continue to draw on for the foreseeable future as new voices join established voices to prove the Arabic saying "Poetry is the mirror of the ages."

Personal Journey

My journey as a poet is not a typical one for a Gulf poet. It began in 2000, after meeting the wonderfully versatile writer, essayist, songwriter, and poet Naomi Shihab Nye, whom I have since called "My Inspiration." I studied English literature, and despite my fondness for Shakespeare, I never attempted poetry, thinking it beyond me and the forte of masters such as Shelley, Lord Byron, Keats, Wordsworth, and Tennyson. Meeting Naomi with her sense of inner peace and calmness, seeing the way she wrote about ordinary people and even such small things as a button or broom, imbuing them with a philosophy of life, made me want to attempt poetry.

For many years I had been a translation specialist, an English writer and reviewer, and I also combined writing with photography. I wrote pieces for international magazines on a range of topics, but I had never tried to write poetry. But meeting Naomi prompted my first four poems on family, and later my first political poem in response to the murder of the young Palestinian Muhammad al-Durrah. This poem became my first internationally published poem.

Following four years of writing poems on women, youth, Arabia, politics, and freedom, I began to compile a collection of poems. During that time I contacted poets in the US and Europe, began experimenting with style, and became interested in modern poetry. In addition to the poems of Naomi, I soon become familiar with modern verse through the work of Wisława Szymborska, Czesław Miłosz, Pablo Neruda, Joy Harjo, Maya Angelou, Langston Hughes, Yusef Komunyakaa, Rita Dove, Robert Bly, Carolyn Forché, and Jane Kenyon.

The first time I began to seriously consider publishing abroad, I wrote an email to Naomi Shihab Nye. She immediately responded and detailed the chronology of first publishing in journals, followed by chapbooks, and then *possibly* having a book selected by a publisher. What she stated was the reality that all poets have to live with: it could take many years to publish a book of poetry, if it happens at all.

I began to seriously revise my work, writing and revising sometimes up to fifty drafts per poem. My composing habits have remained the same for many years: I work from midnight until dawn. Some nights poems flooded in while on others, they trickled in. The journey to publishing a full-length collection took an unexpected turn. I wrote a letter to a US publisher specializing in the Middle East inquiring about a technical matter unrelated to my poetry. During our correspondence he asked what I was working on. I sent off a few poems, and he then asked to see the entire manuscript. I sent off the manuscript, without even entertaining the possibility that it would be picked up. A day later I learned that my book would be published. That day was the first day in a series of surprising days. Poetry took over my life.

The adventure continued in a very unexpected manner. My book, *The Unfurling*, sold over five thousand copies and had three printings in the first six months. My publisher and I worked on a systematic plan of tours, readings, and speaking engagements, what one heading in the media called a "historic tour": the first time a female Saudi poet would give readings in the US. But before I left for the US, I wanted to hold a book signing in Saudi Arabia. Surprisingly, this had never been attempted, and it led to what was dubbed "a leap in the literary scene in the Gulf," a new phenomenon, as poets and writers of both genders weren't in the habit of meeting with readers in such a fashion. Having a signing in a public setting at the largest bookstore in Saudi Arabia, in the coastal city of Jeddah, was a challenge in terms of logistics, but it proved to be well attended. This was followed by another first: a book signing by a Saudi Arabian poet at a Barnes & Noble bookstore in Washington, DC. The tour ultimately evolved to include a US-wide tour followed by international tours.

The Unfurling has received positive notice and reviews, and was featured by *Newsweek International* and *BBC World News*. The unexpected media attention was a challenge for a very private young female poet from a highly private family in a society where the image of fully veiled women often working behind the scenes is the norm.

My work as a poet and activist also led to being nominated as a Young Global Leader whereby I have been able to combine my own love for the arts, a belief in humanity, and a sense of mission to mentor emerging voices. I have endeavored to be a voice for Arab women and youth; and as such I have been active with issues related to youth and women and have campaigned for causes such as working with orphans, mounting a relief campaign for flood victims, and advocating human rights.

Gathering the Tide, with its overarching themes and the combination of the work of established and emerging voices, is an invaluable resource on the intricate and evolving reality of life in the Gulf and in the Middle East. Above all, this anthology shows how poetry can build bridges in this global world and how we can transcend limits and cross boundaries.

"BECAUSE THE SAND WAS MADE FOR ME ALONE TO SPLASH MY INK THERE": NEW POETRY FROM THE GULF

David Wojahn

In January of 2010 the one hundred and sixty-story Burj Khalifa was dedicated in Dubai. It is currently the world's tallest building, and it is (excepting perhaps the Great Pyramid of Khufu and the Great Wall of China) the most grandiose structure ever built. The renowned American architectural firm of Skidmore, Owings and Merrill was responsible for the building's design, which was inspired in part by Frank Lloyd Wright's quixotic rendering of a "mile high" skyscraper to soar above the Chicago lakefront. The Burj Khalifa – a bedazzling concoction of glass and steel shaped something like a sci-fi movie rocket ship – is a truly visionary endeavor, the brainchild of a figure of unflagging entrepreneurial zeal, His Highness Sheikh Mohammed bin Rashid Al Maktoum. Foreseeing that the Gulf's oil reserves are destined to deplete themselves in the fairly near future, the Sheikh has sought to replace his nation's dependence on crude oil with a new dependence on glitz and tourism. The Burj sits in the midst of a development known as Downtown Dubai, among scores of other skyscrapers, dozens of upscale shopping malls, and a brace of four- and five-star hotels. There is nothing in the world quite like Downtown Dubai; Las Vegas, Hong Kong, downtown LA, the hulking vertical business districts of the American Sunbelt – and, yes, even Manhattan – all look a bit paltry beside it. But Downtown Dubai is at present a vexed place. The worldwide recession which began in 2007 has affected the nations of the Gulf every bit as significantly as it has elsewhere. The Burj could only be completed thanks to the last-minute financial largesse of another Gulf potentate, Sheikh Khalifa bin Zayed Al Nahyan, Emir of Abu Dhabi. And Downtown Dubai? Many of its buildings now sit empty and unfinished.

Interestingly enough, one of the poets represented in the pages this anthology is HH Sheikh Mohammed himself. One of his poems addresses his sons on the occasion of their graduation from Great Britain's

Sandhurst Military Academy, and in it he employs the classic tropes of a proud father. His sons are "the dreams of a bright tomorrow." Downtown Dubai is inspired by a vision that is similarly glittering and bright, even in its vast excess. And there's something about Dreaming Big that is as irresistible to the North American mind as it is to the Sheikh and his fellow grandees. That the Burj Khlaifa in some ways fulfills the grandly tumescent dream of Frank Lloyd Wright, perhaps our most insistent, most cranky, and most imperious dreamer, seems altogether fitting. But, as North Americans know quite well – and as the inhabitants of the Gulf states have recently come to know – Big Dreams can only be fulfilled in decidedly fraught ways, and with manifold consequences that are largely unintended. You may get the money, the Long Island mansion with its stables and the pool, and everyone may know you as the dashing Jay Gatsby. But you're also Jimmy Gatz, a poor kid from a one-horse Minnesota town. Our longings derive, above all, from contradiction, paradox, and all manner of inherent ironies.

Poetry, too, derives from these forces. They furnish it with both subject matter and form, and eras of tumultuous social and technological change – when the ironies and contradictions go viral – have often begotten great poetry, although such times can be awful to live through. Tu Fu, Li Po, and Wang Wei composed their lyrics during a time of vicious civil war, and it was trench warfare rather than MFA programs that made Wilfred Owen and Robert Graves into estimable poets. The Russian revolution helped to form the mature aesthetics of Mayakovsky and Mandelstam, although that same revolution would in time destroy them. As we read the poems of Gathering the Tide, we sense above all the immense variety of ways in which contemporary poets of the Gulf must confront contradiction and social upheaval. They are fortunate not to live in times as trying as those of the great T'ang poets or of the Russian poets of the early Soviet period. But they surely inhabit a culture of fraught dichotomies. On the one hand, the nations of the Gulf epitomize modernity – theirs is a world of conspicuous consumption, multi-lane highways, Al Jazeera, and the "economic cities" currently under construction in Saudi Arabia. But on the other hand its nations are for the most part rigidly stratified monarchies whose basic governmental structures differ only slightly from those of the city-states that populated nearby Mesopotamia some four thousand years ago. Progressive forces struggle to bring about free expression and gender equality; traditionalism, most recently in the form of the revival of Islamic fundamentalism, continues to resist these trends.

Yet it is reductive to see this struggle in black and white terms. It is better to say that the poets represented in this anthology have chosen to follow Keats' example as he stated it in his famous Negative Capability letter. They must be "capable of being in uncertainties, Mysteries, doubts, without any irritable reaching after fact & reason." This is never an easy task.

But it is a task made easier for Gulf poets because of the richness of the literary tradition which is at their disposal. The oldest written poems in Arabic are roughly contemporaneous with the Koran, which was set down in the early seventh century. After the spread of Islam beyond the Arabian peninsula in the following century, poetry flourished in the courts of the Abbasid Caliphate in Damascus and the later Umayyad dynasty in Baghdad, as well as in the cities of Moorish Spain. Poetry in classical Arabic is a vital and various literature, notable for its sonic and metrical resources and written in a myriad of genres – there are narratives and epics, devotional lyrics as well as erotic ones.

Although the Golden Age of Arabic poetry in effect ended with the Mongol sacking of Baghdad in 1258, a strong poetic revival took place in the nineteenth and twentieth centuries. Beirut and Cairo became literary centers which in the Arab world were comparable to New York and Paris in the west. They were the locales where the vernacular of modernism was formed, and the writers of the Gulf states have inherited this tradition, one that is much akin to modernism in the west, characterized by a loosening of traditional forms, an emphasis on demotic language, and a cosmopolitan aesthetic breadth. And the Islamic world has produced several contemporary poets of world stature, among them Syria's Adonis, Palestine's Mahmoud Darwish, and Pakistan's Faiz Ahmed Faiz (who composes in Urdu).

The reader of these pages will recognize the influence of many of the current literary styles of the West – where many of the poets in the volume have studied or lived for extended periods. Thus one can identify surrealism in the work of poets such as Oman's Saif Al-Rahbi, feminism in the work of the volume's many female poets (most notably Saudi Arabia's Abir Zaki), and a street-savvy lingo that owes something to the Beats in the case of figures such as Bahrain's Qassim Haddad. But the mixture also includes poets – among them HH Sheikh Mohammed – who favor traditional forms and subject matter. And, given that many of these writers live under regimes that are less than democratic, several of the anthology's contributors – I think of Bahrain's Fawzia Al Sindi – offer poems of social protest that recall the work of Brecht or Neruda. The book's poets ascribe to no aesthetic party line; what they do have in common is that all of them write with engagement and sophistication.

There is thus no "typical" Gulf state poet or poem. But certain of the poems in the pages which follow are worthy of special mention, both for the success of their craftsmanship and for their ability to slyly reckon with the ever-changing societies in which these poets live. Witness, for example, this stark and affecting portrait by Bahrain's Laala Kashef Alghata:

Roadside Flowers
He stands by the side of the road,
arms draped with jasmine chains,
he wears a button-up shirt unbuttoned,
exhaustion in his eyes.

His friend sells roses,
long stems, offering up love
or maybe just a chance.

The heat slides over them,
like blindness, dizziness, and dehydration.
They wipe sweat from their brown skin
offer a flower for a dinar,
something to decay,
fill the car with summer smells.

Bloom at night, fill the house
with flowers, slip them a note—
and barter, two perhaps, for one?
And one retreats, depleted.

The other does not even shrug,
hands over his bounty,
slips the half-note in his pocket
weaves between the cars,
vying for another quick purchase
bathed in the glow of the traffic light's red.

No hope, no future, just routine.
The cars drive toward the green.

Like the portraits of the lost souls and disenfranchised who appear in
Rilke's great *New Poems* volumes, Alghata's tone is at once coolly objective
and yet somehow deeply empathic. This balance is achieved through various
small but ruthlessly ironic details – the quietly savage lines about the
flowers for sale being "something to decay,/fill the car with summer
smells"; the nonchalance of the man who remains at the intersection
after his companion has left the scene, and the deadpan closure. The social
criticism is withering but always remains implicit. There is no need to
mention the social injustice that sometimes lies behind the Gulf states'
glitz – an injustice most acutely felt by the vast number of ill-paid foreign
guest workers whose labors allow the glitz to shine. We do not know for
certain if the flower sellers are guest workers or native Bahrainis, but it
is easy to conclude that they are the former. What we do know is that
Alghata handles the scene masterfully. It is also worth noting that she is
the youngest poet represented in *Gathering the Tide,* born in 1990.

Whereas Alghata looks for something like photographic precision
in her work, the writing of her fellow Bahraini Qassim Haddad seeks
something more kinetic, and even his quietest lyrics bristle with movement
and abrupt juxtapositions. His poem "Body" seems to begin in an erotic
mode. "I saw you in a body where stallions moan/and from whose arms
storms emerge," he writes in the poem's opening lines. But soon the
imagery grows unsettling: the "you" of the poem may be a beloved, or
it may represent a group or culture that has been violated and destroyed.
The poem ends on a note of hushed apocalypse, much in the manner of
Eliot's "The Hollow Men":

I saw you among a murdered race
storming with fire and broken glass.
A body raving with love,
a soul neglected by death.

Haddad carries his juxtapositional method to an even greater extreme
in an ambitious sequence of thirty-three sections entitled "Words for a
Young Night," a mixture of skewed aphorisms, compressed haiku-like
observations of the natural world, and brief love lyrics that collide with

sections of dislocation and menace, political sloganeering, and outcries of sorrow and consternation. This unruly mash-up, Haddad implies, is our lot in contemporary culture. Here's a small sampling:

4
They delighted in sleeping
because of the treasures it lay
between their eyes.

. . .

10
To rule = terror to force acceptance.
To oppose = terror to force resistance.
Both seek to grant prosperity to the people
under one power.

11
I am not free to accept.
I am free only to oppose.

. . .

16
She is like a state.
She puts on her make-up
and talks to her mirror,
and never listens to people.

The final sections suggest no resolution to the conditions the poem describes. It ends on a note of dread that brings to mind the closing of Yeats' "The Second Coming":

31
The clicking of my chains fills the place,
I
who claim freedom.

32
My lip trembles now before a word . . .
My lip is defeated.

33
Be prepared . . . the past is coming.

Finally, a poem by Saudi Arabia's Fowziyah Abu-Khalid. Although she does not engage in the overtly political gestures of a poet such as Haddad, her "My Late Hours With Me" manages to be both an *ars poetica* and a wry feminist parable. The poem is furthermore a feat of cunning lyrical accomplishment; Abu-Khalid's skill with imagery allows her the means to both rhapsodize and lampoon the poetic endeavor. It also permits her to empower the female body, at least momentarily. Hélène Cixous insists that the best writing emerges from "the school of dreams," a place we may visit but never dwell in. Abu-Khalid describes such a visit, and she is always aware that her stay will be brief. The poem's opening passage is an unassuming tour de force:

> By five in the morning, I'm always down to the final drop
> of the night's river in the glasses of the late hours still with me
> All I want then is to sleep for one more hour
> before the alarm rings
> and pulls me by my eyelashes to work
> With no appointment and no prior warning
> there's a knock at the door
> I barely hear it as sleep wrings me out
> and I fall back to sleep
> but the knocking doesn't stop
> The poem climbs to my windows
> by the tendrils of my nerves
> furtively stretching to it
> and it sprays its oil on my fingers
> scatters its burning candles
> on the bed . . .

Abu-Khalid's metaphors are never less than pyrotechnical — "before the alarm rings/and pulls me by my eyelashes to work" is an image of startling ingenuity. But even more noteworthy is her ability to set forth the speaker's decidedly mixed feelings about her nocturnal visit from the muse. The speaker craves her shut-eye; inspiration can wait. The situation is initially portrayed as a comic one, but by the end of the passage I have quoted we understand that the muse cannot be refused. As the poem concludes, the character of the imagery has changed from wit to urgency, and finally to a tone which – somewhat sorrowfully – resolves the poem's warring emotions. Surely this poet has entered the school of dreams, but just as surely she has been forced to leave it:

> And what sort of ink chooses now
> to mix with my blood unaware I've just returned from the sea
> and have already locked in my veins enough topaz, coral, and waves
> I hide from myself in the feathers of a poet
> because the sand was made for me alone to splash my ink there
> But we leave the room together
> to let the woman take off her night clothes
> and bring her daytime self to the mirror

In North America it has become tiresomely fashionable to characterize poetry as marginalized, effete, irrelevant. Our poets themselves claim to be indifferent to such accusations, but I suspect that in most cases these assertions are really bluster. American poets may not today crave monuments (whether they come in the form of High Modernist epics such as *The Cantos*, *Paterson*, and *Notes Toward a Supreme Fiction* or of skyscrapers one hundred and sixty stories high), but I am fairly sure they would like poetry to play a more central role in the culture of the future. It is impossible to predict what that future culture will look like, but we can be certain that it will be a highly globalized and diverse one. And the example of poets who dwell beyond our borders – poets such as those we encounter in *Gathering the Tide* – may help us to see our own poetry anew, and to begin to restore it to the crucial position in society where it properly belongs. Is this a quixotic "dream of a bright tomorrow"? Perhaps. But the outcome remains to be seen.

POETS FROM BAHRAIN

The Kingdom of Bahrain is an island country, connected since 1986 to Saudi Arabia by the King Fahd causeway. With a population of just over a million, half of whom are Bahraini nationals and a third of whom are Indian expatriates, it is the smallest of the Gulf nations. For decades a British protectorate, in 1971 Bahrain gained its independence and is now a constitutional monarchy ruled by the Al-Khalifa family. While its primary source of income is oil, it is also a worldwide center for Islamic banking.

QASSIM HADDAD was born in Bahrain. He did not complete his secondary education, and is largely self-educated. Haddad rose to fame both as a poet and as a revolutionary, and he has written many poems on political subjects dealing with freedom and progress. His first collection, *Good Omen*, was published in 1970, and to date he has published more than sixteen books in Beirut, London, Bahrain, Morocco, and Kuwait, including *Walking Guarded with Ibexes* (1986) and *Qassim's Grave* (1997). He published *Majnun Laila*, a book of poetry and paintings, and also *Azzawi* and *Blue Impossible*, volumes of poetry with photographs taken by the late Saudi photographer Saleh al-Azzaz. Haddad is the chairman of the Bahraini Association of Writers, which he co-founded.

POETS

Translated by Khaled Mattawa

Poets draw nature before it prefigures itself
and they invent
and build a hut abandoned by a gang of thugs.

They sing sometimes
and they form a road so water can take the shape of a river.
They instill in mud the memory of the trees.
A bird discovers its colors in the phrases of a poem,
and picks its rare name.

When poets leave sleep behind
the young thugs begin their rampage.
They romp a little
and they throng as if nature is ambushing them.
They storm and they thunder.

And their limbs begin to thin as if the seasons
were all about to start,
as if childhood selected its shapes suddenly,
and eyes
gaze only at the perseverance of nature.

And the young thugs commit their sins
sip by sip
the way poems clash against the triumph of time.

Creatures offer gifts
and take their tempting shapes
as if a tongue
        made creation. And people,
still startled by their inception,
face the thin ice adorning their mirrors to see
what the poets have done to our feeble dreams.

Poetry maligns speech
and the young thugs commit forgivable sins
the way an infant scratches a breast then weeps to it
the way a text breaks its intentions.

Then the apple of love descends
enamoring a woman with a lost lover,
the way the wolf divulges the myth of the bloody shirt
and the innocent brothers confess their crime
and nature forgives a careless creator
                then praises him.

STONE
Translated by Khaled Mattawa

No one knows stone like me.
I seeded it in the fetus of the mountain,
and I reared it on blossoms of metal.
It grew like a walking child
and I followed in its footsteps.
Its silence is a listening heart
and its solitude is an alphabet that teaches speech,
a burnishing that suffices for treasures,
and imprints itself on books and mirrors.
I read in it the glass of paradise, and the amulets of passion.
It rises lightly, and offers the wind the company of books,
like me.

Solitary, and a companion to strangers.
Its water is the wakefulness of pinnacles.
It guards the sleep of trees, and bends.
At every slope it has an envoy washed by snow,
that it takes from the sea the messages of the waves.
With eyes that exude yearning in a stranger's childhood,
and chased like a tiger swinging in nets that dangle about me,
it listens to the pulse in arteries.
It glows and lusts, roves
and raves,
        like me.
It knows secrets and scandals,
is well-versed in the unseen
The rose takes from it its purpose, and it gazes from the mountain
as the sky discloses and dissolves it shapes.

Like me
its names are in metals
    and in the adversary's alibi.
Like me,
a lover melting, its water is anxiety and the paradise of loss.
It endures love
    and is filled with travel and desire for ecstasy,
like me.
It alone knows the history of my steps and my errors.
It forgives and forgets
               . . . like me.

THE FRIENDS THERE
Translated by Khaled Mattawa

Friends
weave their new rags
in a morning with a missing sun.
Their bodies convulse, and their fingers are caught in a fever of work.
They spin language with the excitement of magicians
and the confidence of
artisans.
They offer wool to summer, and ice to winter.

Friends east of the water,
they work well in solitude.

I stand on the shore.
I watch their silhouettes outline the horizon.
I send them books in bottles that expunge my words.
and they are exceedingly gentle with them.
They run on a bridge
with flaming feet
and there
they climb burdened with scrolls,
a bridge that praises geography and disparages history
and vigilantly watches against the written word.
They hold texts under their arms
and descend like goats decorating the road.
I embrace them.
They cross through terror.
Their memories are of blood,
and their fingers, fastened to glass shards,
are soiled with hacked hearts.
We crash in the midst of love and death

like waves churning salt and luring vessels.
Naked bodies of young men,
where a shirt is never woven for summer,
and no feast is prepared for winter.
The lonesome friends are there.

BODY

Translated by Khaled Mattawa

I saw you in a body where stallions moan
and from whose arms storms emerge.
Abandoned to sighs
trampled by fillies with the whinnying of desire
and the infatuations of mating,
words issued from you like a reed tucked
between sadness and steel.

I saw you among a murdered race
storming with fire and broken glass.
A body raving with love,
a soul neglected by death.

A PRAYER FOR TRAVEL

Translated by Khaled Mattawa

Dear Love, my friend,
place your hand on her heart
as she travels and when she settles.
Offer her dreams when she sleeps,
and give her comfort.
For there is much love in the world
and there is a stranger awaiting her,
unbearably alone.
And there is night, all of it.
And there is much that cannot be described
And there is much that cannot be told.
              Dear Love, my friend.

THE CAFÉ'S MEMORY
Translated by Khaled Mattawa

Your café is waiting for you,
meets you with its befuddled chairs
coming from the forest.
Fresh wood is waiting for your   thick fatigue
massaging your thighs and knees with its soft sticks
and looping your ankles with pliable reeds.
It embraces you   and you forget.
Your café   lonely like you
lonely without you
forgotten on the solitude of the sidewalk
crowded with dreams of waiting and loss.
Its wounds blazing at the nonchalance of the passersby,
it stares at their foot-tread
waiting for a hand to touch its bereft arms.
Your café
waits for you
          like a forest thick with the birds of solitude.

WORDS FROM A YOUNG NIGHT
Translated by Khaled Mattawa

1
We are not an island,
except to whoever sees us from the sea.

2
Wine in half the cup,
the other half was not empty;
it was lost in ecstasy . . .

3
To write
is to breathe unused air.

4
They delighted in sleeping
because of the treasures it lay
between their eyes.

5
I write about love
the way a child draws his impressions of adulthood.

6
An impossible dream
is kinder than a rampant delusion.

7
The curtain on the window
is an orderly more powerful
than his sultan.

8
A vessel between water and fire,
an enticement for flames.

9
He counted his friends to me
on the fingers of his hand.
Then I realized
that his hand had no fingers.

10
To rule = terror to force acceptance.
To oppose = terror to force resistance.
Both seek to grant prosperity to the people
under one power.

11
I am not free to accept.
I am free only to oppose.

12
I see the wind playing with the banner
of this place,
while people go without air.

13
A space crowded with answers.
Everyone is besieged with answers.
Answers in every corner,
and in everything
there are questions.

14
He wants to apologize,
not because he was an enemy
but because he revealed himself as one.

15
Pigs are useful too.
They sing about the garbage bins.

16
She is like a state.
She puts on her make-up
and talks to her mirror,
and never listens to people.

17
All this night
is not enough for my dreams.

18
Every day
we do nothing but confirm the futility
that has been impossible to detect.

19
Usually
I let my memory graze on its own . . .
To forget the wound and remember the knife.
Experience has reached its peak,
and memory is now fatigued.

20
The future
is said to be the opposite of the past,
and we are in an endless present.

21
I have many secrets.
I study them in my poems
and I toss them in the air of language.
Someone has to expose them.

22
This person I do not know
and who does not know me,
why is he so late in arriving
leaving me
to the loneliness of the sidewalk.

23
The children grind their teeth,
and grind with their hearts.

24
Night,
you are not alone.
There are countless other hermits.

25
I look at them;
they are ready to change their stances
by simply shuffling their shoes.

26
They meet to dialogue
and they exchange points of view
the way they exchange masks.

27
Silence . . .
is a flagrant accommodation of folly.

28
You will not convince him with words
if he is not convinced by reality.

29
Before you sleep
place a rose on your chest.

30
What is the difference . . .
between someone blind
and someone who does not want to see.

31
The clicking of my chains fills the place,
I
who claim freedom.

32
My lip trembles now before a word . . .
My lip is defeated.

33
Be prepared . . . the past is coming.

FAWZIA AL SINDI was born in 1957 in Manama, Bahrain, and holds a degree in commerce from the University of Cairo. She has published six collections of poetry in Arabic, including *Akhir Al-Mahab* [End of the Horizon] (1998); *Malath Al-Rooh* [Refuge of the Soul] (1999), and *Rahinat Al-Alam* [Hostage to Pain] (2005). Her poems have been translated into several languages, and she has attended poetry and literature conferences and workshops in the Middle East, Europe, and North Africa. Al Sindi has been a columnist and a contributing editor for a number of periodicals and magazines, including *Kalimat* and *Al-Bahrain Al-Thaqafeya*, and she is a member of the Bahraini Association of Writers. She is well known as an activist, and is among the first Bahraini women who sought their education abroad.

AWAKENING

Translated by Joseph T. Zeidan

1
Awaken, O boughs of passion,
saddle the winds with your exhausted words.
Awaken, like roots craving the taste of salt,
like an echo wandering on a rainy night.
Who is there awaiting the bitter drug
of the streets? The dangerous embers of life . . .
Stare and you will see in me a mirage that sleeps
and awakens with the desert's sun.
My limbs are exhausted from the cold sun
panting after the dead stone.
O, frigid stone, my limbs
pierce me, they are enflamed
by a bewildering chill like the strong arms

of a future nation.
My limbs are openly gouged by death.
They resist, like the panting palm trees in this land,
this saline land.
They resist and I beseech this panic
              to leave . . .
(The roads are a lighthouse,
the climate of alleys in bygone cities,
mazes for those who can't see the dreams of the poor on these walls.)

2
Awaken, for a sweet numbness gathers in my limbs and sharpens me
like a spear plunging in the heart's folds, exploding arteries
of words. Awaken, my voice is not capable of whispering.
It weeps blood,
the perfume of the seventies,
its comrades haunted by stabs
of doubt. I read only the soil
of the past, my blood is taken from me.
It awakens before birth . . . abandons me.
I search a sinful time for blood that haunts me,
for a diaspora that knows the taste of estrangement.
My homeland flees from me.
Who among you has not felt
the ache of blood? Has not questioned
the secret of the flow that secures the heart
on its throne?
I awoke to ask:
who among you?

3
Converse with me, smug time!
Shackles have baptized my limbs with murderous rust,
with doubt, and they have alienated me
in my homeland.

Awaken, O handful of wind known as home.
Bind up your grief.
The bullet kills
if I do not expel your thirst
. . . the bullet kills
if I do not retain your blood within me.
. . . The bullet is coming
if not . . .

Like the sea, awaken
in waves, or a woman.
In my voice the path of your wound now burns,
My eyes are mirrors of fear, in them
your passion will grow, so awaken.

4
Muhammad wandered
these roads begging for tears,
pregnant with insanity/death.
You were
a child, a rose . . .
A book holding the sea between its palms,
a whiteness delirious with flood, a confession
of gulls, steps gathering rocks, a homeland
on edge, its heart leaping with pride.
He ended up at the guillotine.

5
In my voice you spring like water.
You were the beginning: a night
and you are my lighthouse in all
weather. I passed through childhood.
This is my youth wrapped in timidity,
How can I begin
when panic calls?

6

O, boughs of lust panting in my palm, awaken
on a homeland, or a horizon . . .
You will find my eyes enchanted. I am shaking
with fear and love . . .
Awaken.

FROM *LESS THAN INK*
Translated by Bahaa-eddin M. Mazid, with Patty Paine

Ask any war
of victory
and you will be answered
with mountains of blood,
piles of corpses.

Snow is the memory
of the dead.

Kafka—
a precious stone
perfected by the carving
of a chisel . . .

If I were a stone,
I would ignore
the burning
of every wave that hits me.

The affliction of a wound
is not its share of pain;
it is the body uncovered,
the soul not moving
any further.

It is the string
that stirs the hand
to draw sighs
from vocal chords.
No one can see

ahead in the desert,
mirrors of mirage swindle me,
without a single miracle
beyond the cactus heat,
which like me,
can give refuge
to cries of water . . .

Give me time
to spirit away like a letter
that enjoys more freedom
than I . . .

Give me some time,
chiefs of tribes,
to cover the tent
with my body,
and crown patience
with my soul's
burden.

Insanity is a garden
that reason
moves away from.

The night has burned
every piece of paper,
ashamed of the pencil
that's become
stronger.

I am so tired and worn.
Heal me, you,
where pebbles reach
the road that vanishes

beneath my steps;
hide me so that
I am not
a warship collapsing
under a fire of
pouring ink . . .

Writing is a tigress
passionately burning,
a gift to obey, a clever hand,
a careless arrogance
that ravishes
and sees no harm
in claws that charm . . .

It is the triumph of
a plague, a prophecy,
an outbreak,
a loser's share.
It is the rhythm
of my name

ALI AL SHARQAWI, born in Manama in 1948, is a poet, a writer, and a journalist. His poetry collections include *Thunder in the Seasons of Drought* (1975), *She is the Obsession and the Potentiality* (1983), *Psalm 23: To the Singer's Nectar* (1985), *The Crimson Dining-Table* (1994), and *Ibn Haweya's Papers* (2001). He also writes folk poetry and poetry and plays for children.

FROM *PSALM 23:TO THE SINGER'S NECTAR*

Translated by Lena Jayyusi and Naomi Shihab Nye

1
I will knock three times at the door
My mother will know me, will say
the absent one has returned.

He casts his blue-black eyes beyond the rim of vision
his eyebrow rises
and the heart is constantly watchful.
The street is wider than vision
The hollow feet of time have no edges
Hungry questions shower down
over the bags of relief agencies.
　　　—Who will come tonight?
　　　—How will I sleep?
　　　—Is solitude wide enough for the heart's song?
He stops
　　　Damn this gate!
Between the stab-wound and the blade he saw his blood
a Bedouin child on whose lips the horses of daily blows
　　　rest their hooves
and the smell of death leaves its traces

Is there anyone who knows which seas inhabit
    the heart of a prisoner released in the fifth summer?

He turns around
and the gate stands asking
    four?
    two?
    three?

He stops.
The one who passes through this gate turns to stone
and the one who leaves may . . .
The fifth summer scratches the memory of the Bedouin child—
the river abandoned him, wild deer nurtured him.
My heart is taut
My mouth constricts my tongue
and the street – how wide it is!
It stretches from
the tears of a mother's farewell
    to the artery of the fifth summer
I hear her ripe tears crying out
    —Who is at the door?
The fisherman kneeling over the carpet
    comes out to the broken steps
    —Here you are at long last!
I can smell the familiar pledges of neighborhood women.
My soul is contagious with questions
and my aging skin penetrates the new air.
    The gate crouches
        Do not say no.
        Do not say no.
        Do not say it.
He turns—
    what time is it now?

He feels his pocket, removes his watch, and laughs
        It's still telling the time of
the first summer!
He puts his watch away
        Why hurry?

2
Between the lover and love is a wordless road
crossed only by the spirit

3
How can I face my days?
How to live with them
        when the neighborhood is no longer a neighborhood
        a gray sea is buried in my glass
        and all my friends' concerns have changed.

4
From where has this tawny woman sprouted?
Radiant, she emerges from the sea's foam, singing
followed by waves and boats,
by birds escaping the cages of bewilderment,
and by the scorching summer.
Flaming pomegranate trees
        give praise at her feet
walking proud and disdainful as the sun moves over
the Bedouin map.
She swings her childlike laughter
        into the pastures of dreams.
At dawn, where darkness threads with light,
        the lotus tree keeps her company,
        the bird gives her new words.
. . .

6

He stops, swallows his Adam's apple,
stares at the gate remembering slain comrades
    who tried to escape
He walks on.
He eyes the cup of death in the guard's hands.
The cup will make its rounds,
and the axe's teeth will find the soil.
He walks on,
    inhaling and exhaling like other people,
but inwardly seething.
    No one recognizes me
    or if they do
    they ignore me

I left my hands and followed her
I left my blood and followed her
till we met
and I planted my flaming years on her lips
—Mujanar, is that you?
    Where are you going, Mujanar?
    —To where my love is
    —And where might he be?
She departed with violet fragrance on the wings of space
    —There, beyond wishes and prison songs.
And she bade me no farewell.

. . .

9

I perfect the dream and I know
that whoever perfects the dream of the sea
does not drown in a pool of water.

10
The street is congested with foreign languages
    hard on the ear
Has he taken a wrong turn and arrived at Babylon?
Understanding nothing, his steps are painful
as salt in a wound
He is afraid even of himself
    Am I really walking in the streets
    without a policeman?
Advancing gradually as an ant hauling a grain of corn
his feet stutter
A truck could run over him!
How comic death by truck would be
after five years of darkness!

11
I am a sand grouse
and the bustards have hunted me
since the time when I said the old passes away
and desert houses are made of glass.

. . .

14
He advances–
He imagines her preoccupied just now
Fancies possess him,
he follows her fearless steps
The deep waves know her
and the mountain tattooed with trees
She walks like the chant of seagulls
bound to the blood of sailors
She sits happily in the heart of things
On the lotus tree a sparrow
trills his moonspun joy

Mujanar is everywhere – in cells and mirrors,
in rivers and corners
Mujanar, walking in the dark
singing for the day.

. . .

17
Everyone races
Everyone moves like cats toward fish
Everyone munches from another's shoulder
Every step is compulsive
Be my companion, heart
Soften my questions
My memory has aged in the past four years
The muse ran away from me
        And what about the friends?
        Will they come tonight?
We can laugh at our old troubles.
Will my broken mother serve me joy
        baked with laughter?
Will my father tell the familiar story of his first voyage?
I walk forward through the neighborhood . . .
How often I repeated to friends
that I would walk barefoot on asphalt
crying, "Harbor of the world, I am the boat!"
I stare at things, the old playground speaks,
–Have you come to break your hand a second time?
I walk on.
        Should I stop by the coffee bar?
Black tea used to be fragrant and full in the cups
Unrehearsed poetry gushed out from our lips.
        But where *is* the coffee bar?

18
The fifth summer – questions feverish as typhus
    Will I write again?
    Where will I work?

19
I look for her arms
for her purity amidst questions and answers
I walk in the alleyways where children draw
with coal and almonds on the walls
    fish-shaped stars
    cloudlike words
At the end of the line she stood watching me
I approached like Solomon's hoopoe-bird
–Where are you going, Mujanar?
–To the sea, as close to me
as a mother's milk-rich breast
–And what is its color?
–The laughter of Bedouin coffee
–Mujanar?! Perhaps we will meet again
–When you shall speak out!
And she bade me no farewell.

. . .

21
I befriended the darkness,
the moon inside a hole in the damp walls.
I advanced toward a group wearing Bedouin clothes
but recognized no one.
One of them might remember me, I thought,
for my memory is weak in the fifth summer.
I raised my hand saying, "Greetings!"
swallowed my pain, and knocked at her door.

22
I await this maritime girl
to cleanse my bewilderment and outline my path
Who will extract her from my memory?
Who will implant her within my memory?

BEYOND LANGUAGE
Translated by Hameed Al Qaed

Speech has a third hand
Seven lungs
Five eyes
Speech has a mouth
Similar to that of a wolf at the moment of devouring
Weaving an opinion of drought
In a memory
That is speeding now
Between what has happened and what will come
Speech has a speech
That is pursued in a mirage
By the imagination of the first clay
Bridled by family weakness
And is released
Like reindeer within the hills of insanity

HAMEED AL QAED, born in Bahrain in 1948, is a poet, writer, and translator. He has published three collections of poetry: *Lover in the Era of Thirst*, *Noise of Whisper*, and *Alimentation of Violets*. *Noise of Whisper* included poems in Arabic and translations by Al Qaed into English, and won first prize in the 2003 Distinguished Book competition awarded by the Ministry of Information in Bahrain. In 2007, he compiled and translated *Pearl, Dreams of Shell* (Howling Dog Press, US), a collection of work from twenty-nine contemporary Bahraini poets. He has published extensively in Arabic newspapers, magazines, and periodicals, and has participated in many poetry readings and conferences in Bahrain and overseas.

OBSESSION

Translated by Hameed Al Qaed

learn how to hide your secrets
behind the cage of your chest
so no wind hears
learn not to tell your love to your brothers
so they will not become your enemies
learn all names but keep yours to yourself
all those present lost
their upper reach
to an addiction to bowing
to a floor that rejected their faces
learn how to walk on a hair
stretching from sky to earth
without falling
learn how to fight with the arrows of your eyes
without swords
without horses without tongues

and remain victorious
learn while you are running to look back
there are thousands like Brutus waiting
erecting barricades of death
behind your neck inside your body
even in your sleep
protect your back with cement
or better, with steel

PAINTING
Translated by Hameed Al Qaed

⳦

on the bottom:
a deep dark abyss
with its legs open
to pull me down
in the middle:
a shining sword seducing me
a broken heart
containing a bloody world
slipping out of my mouth
on top: a glowing light
pulling back quickly I extend my hand fully
to hide in it
far away . . .

VERSES

Translated by Hameed Al Qaed

1
I will hide our love behind the sun
for no ill wind to find
I will hide it inside a flower
so it remains fresh as your eyes
oh, my beguiling transparent lady
you have stolen the best of my soul
and left me alone

2
she gave me passion
I gave her writings
she was not a woman . . . no
not even a cloud
nor a child
a dead body
or a mummy
she was not a woman
believe me
I don't know myself
at the moment of writing

3
am I stepping from my death
or proceeding to it
I am the revival king
whose blood never betrays
does the water die of lust to a flower
does the heart close
when it finds itself overfilled

with passion the wild rage of youth
oh, fading lust
how cruel you are

4
Hanging with a thread of saffron
between the dream
and the moment just before
wakefulness
the moment whips me awake
the dream holds stubbornly . . .
like one cigarette after another the dream turns to ash
agitated by wind

5
In the battlefield my body fought me
I fought him
and since I was holding my sword
I was knocked down
a victim of a body

AHMED ALAJMI was born in Bahrain in 1958. He is a member of the Bahraini Association of Writers, which he directed from 1999 to 2001. He also served as the editor-in-chief of its journal, *Karaz*, from 2007 to 2009. He has published twelve books of poetry from 1987 to the present, including *Nasl al-Masabih* [Unraveled of Lights] (1990); *Masa fi Yadi* [An Evening in My Hand] (2003); and his latest, *Ka'anahu al-Hubb* [As If It Is Love] (2009), which was published as a set of postcards in both Arabic and English. His work has been translated into several languages, including Spanish, Farsi, French, and English.

MORNING IN PARIS

Translated by Hameed Al Qaed

Just as the cold breeze
Combs the lashes of Paris,
I rest my steps
On the banks of light.
Alone,
I awaken the Champs-Elysee.
I provoke the curiosity of windows
That wish to keep its secrets.
I am unsure,
Perhaps my shoes
Will attract the stares
Of the semi-nude man on the third floor.
Or I might incite the wonder of Louvre creatures.
I am now approaching
The neighborhood
Where the heavens emerge.
Perhaps I can find a poem lost by Baudrillard

Or spy a sin committed by Sartre.
With the same attention
I listen
To the remains of conversations
Left by teens the previous night.
And now, I have no proof
That I was with Cezanne.
See, the silence is diminishing.

ENJOYMENT
Translated by William M. Hutchins

Who among you
Saw me yesterday
When I was overjoyed?
Especially
As my fingers caressed
My son's lustrous hair
And wove with it tales
Of butterflies and foxes!

LAALA KASHEF ALGHATA of Bahrain was born in 1990. When she published her first book, a children's novel titled *Friendship in Knots* in 2003, she became the first Bahraini to publish a book in English, as well as the youngest to publish a book in any language. Her second book, a collection of poetry and prose titled *Behind the Mask: A Folded Heart*, was published in 2006. Kashef Alghata has published poetry in international magazines, both online and in print. In 2007, she founded *Write Me a Metaphor*, an online poetry journal.

REGARD ME SADLY

℠⊃

People or stars
Regard me sadly, I disappoint them
                    —Sylvia Plath, "Sheep in Fog"

The stars nestle deeper
into the sky, throwing
occasional light my way,
sometimes-brightness,
sometimes-beauty.

They are embroidery
on the blanket of the sky,
they are its splendor.

From their fixed places,
from their warmth,
they judge me with sad hearts,
diminish themselves
as I am not worthy
of their magnificence.

The stars nestle deeper
into the sky, on the brink
of disappearing,
as I hurtle further away
from expectations.

I wish to steal the wisdom
of their hearts and step
on the sadness in their eyes
until it is flattened and gone.
I wish to gain redemption.

The stars regard me sadly,
whispering in comets
across the skies, reaching heaven
with their distress.

ROADSIDE FLOWERS

He stands on the side of the road,
arms draped with jasmine chains,
he wears a button-up shirt unbuttoned,
exhaustion in his eyes.

His friend sells roses,
long stems, offering up love
or maybe just a chance.

The heat slides over them,
like blindness, dizziness and dehydration.
They wipe sweat from their brown skin
offer a flower for a dinar,
something to decay,
fill the car with summer smells.

Bloom at night, fill the house
with flowers, slip them a note—
and barter, two perhaps, for one?
And one retreats, depleted.

The other does not even shrug,
hands over his bounty,
slips the half-note in his pocket
weaves between the cars,
vying for another quick purchase
bathed in the glow of the traffic light's red.

No hope, no future, just routine.
The cars drive toward the green.

ALI ABDULLA KHALIFA of Manama, Bahrain writes in both vernacular and classical Arabic. In a career spanning over forty years, he has published eight collections of poetry, from *Anin as-Sawari* [The Whine of the Mast] in 1969 to *Ala-Kalb Wahid* [With One Heart] in 2007. He has published three other collections in French translation, and has collaborated on three operettas. A student of folklore, especially that of the Arabian Gulf, he has held over a dozen folklore-related governmental and quasi-governmental positions. He has founded publishing houses and literary magazines and has received several awards and prizes for his literary work. He also holds honorary doctoral degrees from Giuseppe Colonna University, Italy and the International Academy Orient-Occident, Romania.

THE CLOVER FLOWER

Translated by Salma Khadra Al Jayyusi

I hold your love up as a lantern. The blackness of night
hurts my eyes. The windows of the tower are locked
against my heart.
The lovers' caravans are leaving. My black tents
remain, though the well is dry, the valleys
won't turn green this year,
and the desert was not a witness to our wedding.
At dawn, the cooing of pigeons is a torment,
the face of wind is dusty,
taking me by surprise, and snatching away
a memory that began to wake.
I carry her, my beloved, in my heart
where she moans, wounded . . .
And the clover flower complains . . . Nobody
will bandage its cheeks in the meadow;

the lookout men were watching open-eyed
from behind the fence of thorns
and nobody's left—
only seven slaughtered years and
the flash of a star.

My hands grope the rocks, which rise out of the sea,
the waves gasp. On top of the tower
a lookout coughs and leans
gazing out placidly at the far-off rim.
Because the sea has no
key to the iron coffins
and the rocks are fixed to the sea bed, and the poor
clover flower is calling, breathing fragrance
out from inside the walls,
the hunting hawk unties his leather mask,
terrifying his master,
and soars off beating at distances,
daring the wilderness. The season
of the hunter has not come.
Instead, all creatures are marks for lightning;
in the crane a forgotten promise stirs again.

IN THE PRESENCE OF THE ONE I LOVE
Translated by Hameed Al Qaed

I sit beside the sea of your light.
One evening in the silence of night,
An autumn of songs
Was spreading over the horizon, a thread of a smile, a wisp
    of weeping.
A sob of age, it appears as laughter,
But it is not laughter, it is pain, it is bleeding.
You are a solemn vow, hidden in everything.
Shining like light, your sword brings light,
Brightening us, and your heart belongs to the face of a prophet.
Change in the bitterness of time, the taste of giving . . .

In the dark I open outlets to you
So I may contemplate your secret
Sometimes my soul is orphaned by agony
Other times, tormented by the pain of negligence
I listen in reverence while you play
A chord that never sleeps
I feint like a clever sword
I gaze, you are there calling
My heart is immersed in your light
I come awake,
Drawn to possibility
by a flock of steenboks

No One

Translated by Hameed Al Qaed

In my stormy night, by my heart I see, as one who sleeps,
That I am a tree in one country
With roots in another,
That I am a stone of corundum in its covert place,
That I am a pearl amongst hidden shells,
That I am a bashful wave that gathers clouds
Created by the eternal topography,
That I trigger lightning and melt like hailstones.
I am a stingray seeking the possibilities of birth.
I am a quake of steenbok, fugitive,
The grief of a fallen and withered heart

As one who sleeps,
I see that I am the script and the origin of words.
I am superstitious meaning flashed across
    most splendid eternity.
I am the sweet rhythm tapped out on the face of a tambourine.
I see myself as a flower.
I see myself as a palm tree,
As butterflies aflame in passion

I am surrounded by men made of marble
Who find solace in carvings engraved
    on stone,
People in lines
A melody that inebriates the soul: ever eternal
Ladies made of ceramic,

Sinking in seas of musk, odorless.
On the shore there is the sword of a martyr,
Pigeons, a waste of bleeding

As one who sleeps,
I see that I am a bulbul who sang and sang
Then hid itself away,
That I am sinking in prayers of your visage,
My sorrows vast deserts,
That I am your sleepy limbs on the morning
When they prayed and trembled,
That I have become a slave, angel and hostage
        to physical seduction,
That I suffer an agony of torment.
All this is a response to a question made of foam,
That when my longing overflows
I am scattered into pieces over distance.
Distracted . . . I run and run,
Denying all my histories
In the crowd of the universe.
I am no one.

A WINDOW FOR LONGING

Translated by Salma Khadra Al Jayyusi

There, on the highest shelf, you will rest.
Be careful, I want you to settle
between the perfumes and graceful antiques
till the day my hands can reach you
to dust you off,
sweep the longing from your cheeks
and all that waiting may have done to you.

Dazzled lover,
the road of love has changed.
The concerns of this strange age become
a cross on which the beloved dies,
a token for those of no invention.
Wrap yourself in a grave-like silence
and the solitude of a melancholy night.
Tell your soul: these days, emotions are hard as wood,
and you are merely a small concern among many.
All you are is a swing where one rests a moment,
or summer fruit, unexpectedly come to us in winter.

Why then, out of the blazing furnace,
do you exert yourself each evening,
emerging from the moment of fusion,
to coax dream-buds into flowers
and throw open a window for longing,
a window for longing.

HAMDA KHAMIS is a poet and a freelance columnist. Born in Bahrain in 1945, she has published nine collections of poetry. Her poems have been translated into German, Spanish, English, and French, and she has taken part in many conferences and poetry readings in Bahrain and abroad.

POEMS FROM THE COLLECTION *THE BLISS OF LOVE*
Translated by Ayesha Saldanha

To you . . .

Because you
Are half a pearl
And the beginning
Of despair

Each body
Is a universe

Each poem
A female

How should I scatter
This yearning
So it softens the shock of him
In my blood?

℞◌

O goddess
In hidden ages
You created seven heavens
And seven earths
In six days
And you sat gasping
From the effort of creation

℞◌

He and I
Created seven heavens
And seven earths
Each day
And we sat intoxicated
Radiant
Inventing new heavens
And earths

℞◌

You created five continents
For all humankind
Whereas we
From the bliss of love
Create fifty continents
For the gardens of the body

℞◌

Quietly infiltrating
My being
A deep

River—
Your voice!

❧

In your love
I traversed love
And passion
Ecstasy/distraction
Craving/weakness
Enslavement/devotion
. . .
And
O God!
Is there no other
Realm?

❧

Do you remember
The paths
On which we walked?
. . .
They became
My veins

❧

You, alone
Fruit of the soul
The day
And the body
You, alone
My choice
And my despair!

◁⅋▷

Body
With body
Volcano
With volcano
. . .
Doesn't the world burn?

◁⅋▷

I walk with you
My pulse in your palm
The earth, cotton
And saffron

I walk with you
Everything softens
The dust, the asphalt
The heat and noise
My feet are wings
My happiness is downy feathers
Flying in passing faces

◁⅋▷

Who?
    Those?
        Which?
            Surround?
                Me?

. . .

. . .

I can't see
        Anything but you
                Around me!

☙

The ink
My blood
. . .
. . .
And your scent!

☙

When you touched me
Torrents rushed
Through my body
And they still have not
Abated

When you kissed me
The galaxies
Were disturbed
And stars
Fell on my body

☙

Forty years
I searched for you
We met
. . .
. . .
We separated
. . .
. . .
Forty centuries
I will search
For you

The body
The soul
The substance
The idea
Dust
Flame
I
You
Which of us mysterious?
Which of them, clear?

Not once
Did I sit
With a man
Without you sitting
In his place!

Whenever I'm close
To the darkness
Of despair
A mysterious glittering
In your eyes
Illuminates me

Tell me
How
In the span of the one hand

Enclosing us
The whole world
Stands

Alone
I sip your absence
Drop
By drop
And I become intoxicated
When I behold you

COUPLE

Translated by Hameed Al Qaed

Oh, man who has been living
in our home for twenty years.
Why don't you speak to me?
Like a transient
I'll depart
Leaving the room
Full of chatter!

RAY

Translated by Hameed Al Qaed

I do not write poetry
For glory
Nor to seek fame
in the media
I write to illuminate
Like a ray
Sneaking stealthily
To eliminate darkness!

THOSE NOT FOR ME
Translated by Hameed Al Qaed

The present now is
    not for me
The man who showers
Before bathing in my body
    is not for me
The man exhausted by running in my labyrinths
    is not for me
The man who preens
glazing his nails
Before he scarifies my monotony
    is not for me
The man who satisfies those around me and ignores my hunger
    is not for me

These glazed walls
    are not for me
The house heavily armed with normality and familiarity
    is not for me
The house that defines my incarceration
    is not for me
The beautified mare
With her bridles and saddles
    is not for me

❧

Mine is the vast desert
Mine is the shine of dawn
Mine is the youth of the liberated mare
Mine is the reindeer
All glitter is mine and
Mine is the macrocosm!

WITHOUT REASON
Translated by Hameed Al Qaed

Without reason . . .
Writing rebukes us
It commands us
Drives us once to heaven
And another time toward flame . . .
Without reason!

ALI AL JALLAWI began writing poetry at a young age. His early work was characterized by revolutionary and political ideas, and he was arrested at the age of seventeen because of a poem in which he criticized the political regime in Bahrain. He was arrested again in 1995 and imprisoned until 1998. More recently Al Jallawi's poetry has dealt with philosophical and human-oriented subjects. In addition to writing poetry he has completed two novels. He lives in Manama and runs a research center dedicated to writing about Bahrain's minorities and communities ignored by official histories. His website is www.jallawi.org.

ACCORDING TO A CLOUD WHISPERING TO HER SISTER

Translated by Ayesha Saldanha, with editing by Patty Paine

According to my father
According to his neighbor
According to a scarecrow in the field
Accusing the birds
Of not waking the morning
Of shaking the roses
And agitating the dew

According to a cloud sitting on
A shoulder of words that return
Wet with a kind child
Whose neighbors pretend not to see
Plucking apples
From their dresses
And fiddling with cherries

According to my father
According to a seagull under his shirt
Trained in the sea's rituals
I say (to a cloud whispering
To her sister) The boy planted
The poem in a vessel of water
But the girl's hand took
Root on a stone.

You . . .

Translated by Ayesha Saldanha

Go into
The poem's deviation
Or its peace

Everything that is not said
Is poetry.

TRYING TO UNDERSTAND
Translated Ayesha Saldanha

What would happen
If I pretended to be a magician
And placed you in a top hat
Then pulled you out
As doves?

What would happen
If you kissed me by mistake
Then kissed me in apology
For the mistake?

What would happen
If I tried
To put my hand on your chest
Just to search for a moon I had lost?

What would happen
If I reached my hand into your eyes
And pulled out all the seagulls?

What would happen
If you had not happened?
The universe would be thrown
Off kilter, and the poets
Would lose the wolf
Of their wisdom.

It happens
That nothing happens
When you are not there.

THE WISDOM OF HALLAJ*

Translated Ayesha Saldanha

Whenever the heart strives
It commits errors
We know

But
That which is not said by the poem
The prophets understand.

*Mansur Hallaj (c. 858–922 CE): Persian mystic, writer, and teacher of Sufism.

KARIM RADHI was born in 1960 in Tubli village. He started writing in the 1980s, and published his first collection in 2003. He has had poems and articles published in many newspapers and magazines in Bahrain and other Arab countries, and he has also participated in a number of conferences and poetry events locally and overseas. He is an active unionist.

CHIEF OF STAFF

Translated by Hameed Al Qaed

He hides on different corners
And orders others through communication devices
To die
For the sake of what he calls duty

MISSILE

Translated by Hameed Al Qaed

Oh you, the one crossing continents
Halt your conceit
Before you, a slim book
Better written
And less expensive has similarly crossed

NIGHTS OF WAR
Translated by Hameed Al Qaed

The moon does not see us
And has no hands to wipe the smoke
From its face

PRETEXT
Translated by Hameed Al Qaed

Once in the name of freedom
Once in the name of the motherland
Once in the name of nationalism
Once in the name of religion
This war is nameless
It borrows its name endlessly

SOLDIER

Translated by Hameed Al Qaed

Look at him running
A boot wearing a man

WAR MARTYR

Translated by Hameed Al Qaed

He was thrown out of heaven
When the myths
Complained of his odor

WAR POET

Translated by Hameed Al Qaed

He is elated, ecstatic over the large number of people slain
The poem will be a dramatic sensation

WAR REPORTER

Translated by Hameed Al Qaed

CRO

He yearns to reach
the death scene fresh
So his report will be exciting
And the pictures effectual

WAR TRADERS

Translated by Hameed Al Qaed

CRO

How impudent they are
They invited our friend Picasso
To attend a function for revising Guernica

Adel Khozam is a poet, journalist, editor, and broadcaster. He also writes on theater and the cinema and composes music and lyrics for theatre and television. Since 1993, he has published three collections of poetry, a history of visual art in the Emirates, and a history of theatre in the Emirates. He also published the first spiritual book in the UAE, *The House of the Wise Man*, in 2010. Born in Dubai in 1963, he currently lives in Dubai and works as Deputy Channel Manager of Sama Dubai TV.

WHITE SHAME

Translated by Joseph T. Zeidan

The sentence was uttered in its entirety
Why did not you believe it
The sentence?
It just passed in front of you
Or you are the one who passed in front of it.
It just passed in front of you
Or you are the one who passed by it. It does not matter
The sentence?
Do you recall that it
Stung you in the spinal cord?
Do you recall?
Do you recall the love
And the word "clarity"
And the man's first scream and it was: In the name of the breast
of the mother
Yes
And then they told you: This is the world
And said: Be shattered for the sake of the end
Yes

Do you recall
It is the fault that indifference repeats
It is the disease
It is the white shame
Take your shoes and come
Come light, lighter than your shadow
Otherwise come at night
And fall into repetition
It is the fault
It is the disease renewing itself
In your very health

DO THIS
Translated by Joseph T. Zeidan

Take a red rag . . . Place it on your enemies' heads
And then watch the color turn into a symbol
Then, a year later
Beautify the wall with holes
And let the air free
Tell the woman: Love is a buried mirror
Love is evenness
And from time to time
Try to alter the chess of symbols
Or toss in order to hit the emptiness
Perhaps, while tossing, you will split the target
And dismantle the scuffle of two enemies

SLIDING
Translated by Joseph T. Zeidan

❦

I threw half my dreams into the garbage
I put on a shirt and went out
I wandered in the wounded streets
While my statue is with me
I pulled the thread dangling
From the cloud of vision
And then the angels glided
And my entire homeland
Became moistened with dreams

DESTINY
Translated by Issa J. Boullata

❦

Far away
at the edge of the earth
a man stands
and leans over to stare into his abyss
Then comes the ox of memories
and butts him into the emptiness

TRANSIENT LOVE

Translated by Joseph T. Zeidan

Destiny that brought us together
Divided us in the room
Traveled in our manners
Like bad blood
Rebelled
And was thrown back
And broke when we hugged
We were a pair of scissors
And a spot of blood
Caused by an unknown knife
A kiss originally a stab
And a hanged capital
And an Arabism
Dispelled by the barbarism of silence
And between us the fire
And the yellow wood of dignity
And the jam of the holiday
And the stubbornness of the road
All of them
Tied to the thread of joy

THE HEROISM OF A THREAD
Translated by Issa J. Boullata

My enemy will pass after I do
Please help him
Provide his camp with dogs and fresh dates
Open the gate of wind for his soldiers
I don't mind
I have passed through the narrow opening
I laugh
because the one behind me is . . . an elephant

STRANGE CIRCLES
Translated by Joseph T. Zeidan

Then, that was my alienation
To recover the remainders of dignity
Rising above the idea of regret
Jumping with the deceived
Dancing around him
And around myself
Coming while inflicted with absence
Within myself every insight
Is destroyed by doubt
Every pleasure seizes its location
And nothing remains for the body
Except the cause of its escape
I mean here is the cause of the stranger

I describe whomever I describe
The man who piles up the workers
In the shape of a pyramid
The dry woman at the stream
The lame dog at the bus stop
And my mother
And talks about tyranny
Except when I wipe out another one

I reclaim from the stranger
His addresses and ignorance
I treat the adversary harshly
While wrapped with confrontation
But the stranger pulls me by my clothes
To cross the water
To peep on the contrast of meaning

And believe the game around us
So I grabbed the memories of others
I was infatuated and violated my blood
I told the stranger that he owns all the earth

They climbed the ladders and he was with them
They shook the big idol, and he was with them
We were plowing the lake called heart
And leaning against our differences

Together
I walked with the truth while I was alien to it
I believed the road when it
Seduced me with the end
I believed my father
The dogs and the secular people
Why did I come to the place of my farewell?
How did the fire defeat the yearning?
How did my friends evaporate like artificial smoke?
My friends, I take refuge in them
But the stranger decides to trade his mask with me

The raven jokes with the flock of sea gulls
The judges joke with justice
Poking it with a stick
The clown jokes with gravity
Attaching himself to the ceiling
The young girl jokes with her breast
The stranger jokes with death
Receiving and exchanging
The currency of adventure

What is the use of your far away screaming, stranger?
Sanctify your conditions
And follow the hedgehog's advice
Barefooted they bury you
If you hit them with your shoes
You, who talked to them about
The nature of absence and its unknown spheres
About the relationship between body and door
And the rotation of man around the sun
What does your screaming say
Except this whisper?

Come closer, stranger
We will sit down like statues for a moment
We will sit closer to ourselves
Like the statues
A rock facing a rock

Confused in the homelands
One half of me is departure
The other half is a road
I make severe my language
And my oath is violated
I recited songs until my tongue
Turned yellow
And the rug of words slipped
From my mouth
I said;
Alienation is the strength of the weak
So all slipped from my mouth

To whom did you return to plead, stranger?
The exiles dissected you rib by rib
Your opinion got twisted
And the directions of your face became inverted
The eternity that you challenge

Threw you finally to pond of nihility
So take your heart and match
Stab it with treachery
Do not stay in the place
Of your sale

I walk and its shadows follow me
A man is close to his forties
A man standing as if in a circle
He gave my description
And he started turning around
Betting on the tragedy

POETS FROM KUWAIT

The State of Kuwait borders Saudi Arabia and Iraq and is the northern-most of the lower Gulf countries. Its population of about three million includes 1.2 million Kuwaitis and a million Arabs of other nationalities, with the rest of the population primarily comprised of expatriate workers from South Asia. Having gained its independence from Great Britain in 1961, it is now considered a constitutional emirate, ruled by the Al-Sabah family in conjunction with a popularly elected National Assembly. Long a port for trade between India and Mesopotamia, its income today comes primarily from its vast oil reserves. Although it has been somewhat slow to develop following the Iraqi invasion and occupation of 1990–1991, in recent years it has made great progress in improving its educational system, including higher education, and in diversifying its economy.

SOUAD AL-MUBARAK AL-SABAH was born in 1942 in Kuwait as a member of the ruling family. She graduated from the Faculty of Economics and Political Sciences at Cairo University in 1973, and obtained a doctorate in economics from Surrey Guilford University in the UK in 1981. Al-Sabah is the director of the Kuwait Stock Exchange and a member of the Higher Council for Education, the executive committee of the World Muslim Women Organization for South East Asia, and the board of trustees and the executive committee of the Arab Intellect Forum. Her literary publications include *Wamdatt Bakira* [Early blinks] and *Lahathat min Umri* [Moments of my life] (1961). Her scientific works in English include *Development Planning in an Oil Economy and the Role of the Woman* (1983), and *Kuwait: Anatomy of a Crisis Economy* (1984).

A WOMAN FROM KUWAIT

Translated by Nehad Selaiha

1

My friend:
In all Kuwaiti women there is something of the
        temperament of the sea.
You'd do well to study me, before you venture on
        my sea.
My friend:
Don't let my calm deceive you,
For storms can brew behind the mask.
I can be clear and gentle like a lake,
But storm and blaze,
Like a fire.

2
My friend:
I have escaped the contamination of the age of oil,
My faith in God is firm still.
Were you to search the depths of my soul,
You'd find the old black pearls
Deeply planted in its bed.
My friend,
Whom I love to the marrow of my bones,
Everything around me
Is soap bubbles and straw,
So be my sail.

3
My friend,
The Kuwaiti woman, if you get to know her well,
Is a river of love, big and great,
And a cyclone of kohl.
May God protect you from the torrents of my
        perfumes and my kohl.
A Kuwaiti woman can only love you madly.
If this be so, what can you know of what I feel?
In rage, a burning match am I,
In joy, a soft silken thread.
My friend,
A Kuwaiti woman will never speak her love.
When will you read between the lines?
Under my fragrant trees of tenderness, lie down,
And in my incense, bathe yourself.
For in your land my seeds I've sown,
And in your heart my roots have grown.

My friend,
A Kuwaiti woman has let down her night tresses
    like a bridge,
Ignore the guards.
The soldiers,
And the veils,
For she has tired of the clouds and dust,
And all the scorching desert winds,
And longs for the orchard shades,
The music of fountains,
And the song of birds.
The Kuwaiti woman
Is fighting her great battle with history,
The outcome, not decided yet.
Will you support me?
The Kuwaiti woman has named you my prince, my
    prince,
Control the destinies of the ages,
Conduct my fate.

4
My friend,
I am a thousand women rolled into one.
I am the rain,
The lightning,
The music of spring,
The wild peppermint,
The solitary palm tree,
The tears of all the lyres,
The sadness of the mournful sands.

5
My friend,
You who holds in his scarf the light of day and
    loosens it,
Who I would follow till my death, or suicide,
How I have longed that one day you'd be
A ring in my ear, a bracelet around my wrist.

6
My friend,
Out of millions I have picked you,
Applaud my excellent choice.

FEMALE 2000

Translated by Abdul-Wahid Lu'Lu'Ah

Like all the women of the earth
I could have courted the mirror.

I could have sipped my coffee,
In the comfort of my bed.
And on the phone could have practiced chatting,
Heeding neither days nor hours.

I could have minded my beauty,
Applied kohl round my eyes;
And in the manner of a coquette,
Roasted my body in the sun,
And danced, like mermaids on the waves.

And I could have
Twinkled with rubies and turquoise;
Strutted like a queen.

I could've done nothing.
Could have read nothing.
Written nothing, cared for nothing
But the limelight, fashions and travel.

I could've chosen
Not to reject,
Not to rage in anger, nor
To scream in the face of tragedy.

I could've chosen
To swallow my tears,
To swallow suppression.
And be tamed like a prisoner.

I could've chosen to ignore
The questions of history,
The incriminations of self.

I could have chosen to be spared
The sorrow of the down-trodden,
The cry of the oppressed,
The riot of the thousands who have died.

But I betrayed the laws of the female
And chose to fight with my words.

INGRATITUDE

Translated by Abdul-Wahid Lu'Lu'Ah

The child sucks at his mother's breast,
Till he has had enough.
He reads by the light of her eyes,
Till he learns to read and write.
He steals from her purse
To buy a pack of cigarettes.
He walks over her lean bones,
Till he graduates from university.
When he becomes a man,
He sits in one of the elite cafes,
Putting one leg across the other,
And holds a press-conference to say
That women have half a mind,
And half a religion.
Then he is applauded by the flies
And the café waiters.

LOVE POEM 1
Translated by Mohammed Ali Harfouch

Addressing this letter to you,
I expect no reply.
Your reply hardly matters.
My lines are the heart of the matter.
To me, writing dialogue,
Before my dialogue with you.
I can recall your memory
Regardless of your physical presence.
I can also stroke your body,
Though it's not by my side.

Don't delude yourself that I'm an
Idealist,
A mystic,
Or a woman as cool as a cucumber.
However, on paper
I draw your facial features
As I like,
And reshape them at ease,
And flirt with them at ease.
I'm writing
To divert my internal floods
That have devastated all my dams.
To rid myself of this electric charge,
Burning my nerves.
Of these lightning bolts,
Flashing in my veins,
Finding no outlet.

I drop you a line
Not to satisfy your vanity, as you might think,
But rather to celebrate – for the first time–
My birth as a woman in love.
And to let my emotions explode in the face of the world.

Writing
Takes me to an artificial paradise
I cannot enter,
Gives me liberty
I can never enjoy,
Makes me azure isles
I can never reach.
To you, writing
Is a safety valve preventing my explosion.
The only boat I board
When the storm chews me up.

I'm writing
To defend every inch of my femininity
Occupied by colonial forces,
Yet to pull out.
Writing is my weapon
To crack what I cannot break:
The walls of forbidden cities,
And the guillotines of the Inquisition.

I am writing to get rid of myriad squares and circles
Restricting my thought,
To emerge from the belt of pollution
That has poisoned all rivers
And beliefs,
And aborted thousands of books
And intellectuals.

I'm writing to you,
Or to somebody else,
Or to anyone at all.
I want to tell the paper
What I can never reveal to others.
Those others
Have been scheming against femininity
Over the past fifteen centuries.
I want to hack a hole in the flesh of the sky.
My city
Only likes to listen to crows cawing,
Steeds whinnying
And fighting bulls bellowing.

I'm writing
To be free of my masks,
From the olive-and-cheese bundle,*
Carried on my mother's head,
Ever since her breasts appeared.

I'm eager to spill the beans:
It is incredible
That I should love you so fantastically,
Yet I must keep my secret like a fetus in my womb
For fifteen centuries.

I am writing
To get rid of myriad squares and circles
Restricting my thought,
To emerge from the belt of pollution
That has poisoned all rivers
And beliefs,
And aborted thousands of books
And intellectuals.

Yet a woman
Writes
In the same way she would deliver a baby,
With the same enthusiasm
She would breast-feed a baby.

The man writes during his leisure time.
The woman during her fertility,
When impregnated with lightning,
And tropical fruits.

Like a mare
I'll go on neighing upon my papers,
Until I have bitten into the globe,
Like a ripe apple.

*An image of subordination: the Arab woman brings her husband his meal to the field.

MY BODY IS A PALM TREE THAT GROWS ON BAHR AL-ARAB
Translated by Nehad Selaiha

◌෨◌

1
I am the daughter of Kuwait,
Of the sandy shores that slumber
By the waters like a gorgeous doe.
In the mirror of my eyes,
The night stars embrace the palm trees.
From this spot sailed my ancestors in fishing boats,
And came back with the impossible catch.

2
I am the daughter of Kuwait.
I grew up with the pearls of the sea,
And nestled in my lap the shells and the stars.
The sea was kind to me, and Oh! so liberal!
Then came the damned devil of oil,
And all fell prostrate at his feet,
And worshipped night and day.
We forgot the desert ethics, its honor, and
    hospitality,
Our coffee mortars, our ancient poetry,
And drowned in trivialities.
And all that was bright, real and great
Was swept away.

3
I'm the daughter of Kuwait.
Inhabiting the sun,
I number the morning among my surnames.
My forefathers explored the waves, the sea,
And the music of the wind.

They befriended death and tirelessly pursued their
    Dreams,
With horse and sword,
With never a moment's repose.

Then came the curse of oil,
And what was forbidden became common practice.
Our orchards became hot beds of sin,
And the cheap perfume of foreign adventuresses
Filled the night air.
At their feet gold was strewn,
And on their bodies drinks were lined.
Indeed, my countrymen,
This is how a nation should fight!
On the wall, meanwhile,
An antique sword of my fathers hangs weeping.
Even the sword has despaired!

4
My country, I don't know any more!
Are you this land of markets and bazaars?!
Of bouncing checks,
And gambling shops,
And fifty sharks prowling around our seas?
Is this the Kuwaiti people
Slaughtered by the mafia in broad daylight?
Rise up in anger, O my land!
You never fought except with words.
The offspring you brought to the world in long and
    painful labor,
Are now the knights parading in the
    money-changers lane.

5
Rise up in anger
O my land. Long have you slumbered
In your bed of gold.
Rise up in anger!
For gold has made you drunk,
And vanity made you blind.
I won't believe that oil is a fate we can't escape;
No fire-worshipper am I
Who with her children feeds the cursed flame.

My country,
Put down the currencies bulletin, leave the
      stock-exchange
And join the Arab forces.
In Lebanon, children die;
The land is daily raped.
In anger, rise my land!
For only anger tills the land.

6
Sometimes I dream of Salah al-Din
Begging for a crust of bread in the alleys of
      Jerusalem,
Begging at the doors of the knights of Arabia;
Sometimes I see him in the desert,
Lost and wandering, searching for the old tribes,
For Tai, Tamim, and Ghuzayyah,
Or in a police station,
Thrown against the wall without identity or bail.
I, then, cry, from the depths of my wound:
Curse you, age of mediocrity
In which the Arab's sword has lost his identity!

7
I am the daughter of Kuwait.
Whenever I think of today's Arabs, I weep.
When I remember what became of Quraysh,
The Prophet's tribe, after his death,
I can't check my tears, and weep.
When I behold this dear homeland
Racked by oppression and suppression, I weep.
When I examine yesterday's map
And see our map today,
I weep.

Whenever I see a bird in Rome
Or Paris sing
Without fear, I always weep.
And when I see an Arab boy
Sucking hatred at the breast of Arab radios,
I weep.
Whenever I see an Arab army
Opening fire on civilians,
I weep.
And every time a ruler boasts of his people's love,
Of ruling by consensus of opinion, or of the
        freedom of speech
I weep.
Whenever I am questioned about my passport
By some policeman at an Arab port.
I turn my back and leave.

8
I am the daughter of Kuwait.
Could my heart dry up one day
And stiffen, like a wooden hobby horse?
Grow cold and unfeeling
Like a wooden hobby horse?
Can I ever be anything but an Arab?
My body is a palm tree fed by the waters of Bahr
    al-Arab,
And my soul reflects all the errors, all the sorrows,
All the hopes of the Arabs

I shall always keep on waiting
For the Mahdi to arrive,
A singing bird in his eyes,
A shining moon,
And the first drops of rain.
I shall always keep on searching
For a willow and a star,
And the garden behind the mirage.
I shall always keep on waiting
For the flowers that will sprout
Under all these ruins.

GHANIMA ZAID AL HARB was born in Kuwait in 1949, the daughter of Zaid Al Harb, a popular Kuwaiti poet. She has been writing poetry for more than twenty years and has published four collections. A selection of her poems written about the Iraqi invasion of Kuwait was performed as a play during the annual cultural festival in Kuwait.

ESCAPING FROM THE COMA CAGE

Translated by Haifa Al Sanousi

It knocked at my eyelids.
Waking me up,
Half-asleep.
In clouds of hope
Two angels beside me
Rousing me to sublimity.
The clouds' eyes
Spread light, and serenity enveloped me.
The rivulets of veins
Were watered with purity.

And there were eyes–
Drinking fire
In the night of waiting.
Whenever they extinguished one fire
Illusions lit another.

They drugged her
With promises of my coming, and an apology
The night wore out.
She woke up,

Drinking the day's unseen grasp.

Birds behind the sea
Carrying these promises.
When I bid farewell I said:
"I'll be back."
I kept my promises.
In that bereaved night
I crossed the borders,
And awoke.

It is my heartbeat
And all that remains of those seconds
And my longing for life
When I screamed
And the hand of safety
Was extended.

THE SPARKLE
Translated by Haifa Al Sanousi

We are in the time of names
Not that of creativity.
So sing.
Everything in your name
Is marvelous.
Any drum
Any beat
Any letter.
Anything goes
Under your light.
Sing
In this barren time
Of disappointment,
In the age of catastrophe.
Any letter
Will seem sparkling
Under your name's light.

HAIFA AL SANOUSI holds a PhD in Modern Arabic Literature from the University of Glasgow and is an associate professor of Arabic literature at Kuwait University. She travels widely to lead literary workshops and to present academic papers. Al Sanousi has published extensively in the field of literary criticism and is the author of several collections of short stories, novellas, children's books, and training manuals for literature and therapeutic healing workshops. She is particularly interested in the application of literature and storytelling in psychoanalysis and medicine.

IT IS NOT FAIR

I can scream, sing and laugh.
No chains, no bars, no shackles.
I wonder
why people in that part of the world
are screaming for my freedom?
I need to unveil
the minds that refuse
to listen.
But a noise is approaching . . .
A loud voice fighting for my freedom,
While I am here sitting on top
of a mountain, flying
with singing birds
and colorful butterflies.
A smile shines on my face.
I am singing in a different voice.
Will they hear me?
Will they enjoy my song?
I have everything I want.

Will anyone dare open
the curtains of my world?
I am waiting . . .
Waiting . . .
Waiting . . .
I come back home feeling
sorry for myself.
In that part of the world,
no one wants to listen,
and no one wants to budge.
But still I have hope.

BIRTH OF WORDS

Why is it so important
to keep pen and paper in my bag?
Why do thoughts come to me
at strange times? Like today,
in a park crowded with people
my kids were playing in the Wonder
Land when I heard the noise
of a train. The screams
of my children and the screams
of the train mixed
with the scream of words
being born.
Words are always knocking
at the exit, rattling the gates of my mind.
I need to breathe life.
I need pen and a paper,
so from the prison of my mind
my words can be released
to meet you, dear reader,
your soul and mind, only you
are able to absorb their flash.

KHALIFA AL WOQAYYAN was born in Kuwait in 1941. He has been writing poetry for more than thirty years and has published four collections. He also holds a PhD in Arabic Literature.

THE HARVEST
Translated by Haifa Al Sanousi

You! Traveler
Into the journey of worry and dream.
The night has exhausted you
And your feet are bloodied by sharp rocks.
When you walk you break
The stillness of the deserts,
The silence of the sea,
And the calm of the night.
In your rags the tired sleep,
And the frivolous drink you toast.

It is your fate.
You end where peacocks spend the night,
Haughtily they wander. Escape and hide in the mountains
Larks lie in their nests
On eggs of death.

It is fate.
What should not be,
Be.
Spiders go on

Weaving the shroud
of the murdered babe.
Nothing but pitch dark
Hangs over the path.

You alone are
Plowing the sea
Implanting in the wind
All the seeds:
The twitch of dream,
The scent of flowers,
The chirping of birds,
The wheat of ages.

You alone are
Harvesting in the carnival of booty:
The thorns of the grave.

A PULSE
Translated by Haifa Al Sanousi

What do you want?
You, who are always in my mouth,
Like a handful of iron,
Like a piece of ice.
You count my tears . . . and
The flames between my ribs
My smiling and turning . . . and
My heartbeats.

My fingers are cut off.
My bag is lost
My sparrow is in its nest,
Sad and scared.
I have nothing
But this willful pulse.

AN ELEGY
Translated by Haifa Al Sanousi

The newspaper arrives like an owl
With your name in the morning
Telling incredible things about you.
It goes on reporting
Fahad's wedding, Zaid's birth,
And a tea party for a dear guest.
Telling the trivial, worthless news.
I read it once, twice, three times.
They might have made a mistake in your name,
Which is imprinted on my pulse.
But I know your name, your father's name
Your grandfather's name and your family's name.
I try to search for a misprint,
Just to keep you alive,
To kill someone else.
I don't blame my love.

The minutes pass like ages
No sign of you, no call
To kill the fear, the sadness
And the terror.
The paper screams your name.
In every corner the name grows
Filling all the space.
I see nothing now
But the obituary
Screaming, screaming.
It fills my ears.

It squeezes my heart
It blocks all roads.

◌

I want the phone to ring,
to hear your voice and lovely laughter
to hear you gossip
and laugh as you do.
I throw the paper away.
I look for you like a child
To kiss your eyes,
To lament you
Out of joy or out of fear.

◌

Did you really pass away?
Horrendous is the news.

How miserable are our barren days?
Do you leave when the land is thirsty
For the grace of your hand,
Your touch of love,
A glimpse of light,
The break of dawn
On your lips.
Have you gone?
How can we get you
With our chests of grief?
And you are the expert
On the contents of chests.
You were always big,
When we grew small and
Strong when we weakened.

Who now gives power to the inept,
Sweet hope to the desperate?

MOHAMMAD ALMOGHRABI holds a BA in Arabic Literature from the Faculty of Arts, University of Kuwait, and he has served as editor of the cultural section of the newspaper *Arab Times* and as editor of the National Council for Culture, Arts and Letters' *Journal of the Arts*. His publications include the poetry collections *On recent thresholds* (2001) and *Obi and in your face and go to bed* (2004), the long poems *Outside of the biography of death* (2005) and *Is the rain* (2007), and the novel *Leg throne* (2007). He is a member of the Association of Writers in Kuwait, and is a regular participant in poetry festivals in Kuwait and throughout the Arabian Gulf.

THE MURAL OF ARROGANCE

Translated by Khaled Al-Masri

To Amina's soul

The world is a
wasteland,
a wasteland is my destiny.

Mother, they took you and the earth covered you.
Who will soothe your heart when you descend
into the grave with no acquaintance or companion?
You call me. I know your heart
ached when my foot stumbled on the front steps
You hastened to dress my wound.

Who will soothe your heart
when the floods engulf you?
You no longer say to me "anything for you"
O my faraway mother,

only you understand the foolishness of my fugitive smile.
"Anything for you"
O my faraway mother,
only you braid the dreams on my pillow and calm the lonely cats.
"Anything for you"
O my faraway mother,
only you are in my blood. You are my sense of belonging, a psalm in
my book of scriptures, a rhyme in the cameleer's song, my armor and
my fledgling steps forward, my rapid race to the sunset, the wing of
my demanding soul.
"Anything for you"
O my faraway mother,
night's laughter strikes me and scatters its salt in the eye of my wound
Talk to me
My heart scaled its fence so as to snatch a glimpse of your eyes,
to embrace you,
to further burden you with that which weighs heavily on the arms.
My heart was a beggar at your door, pleading glances and words.

Your voice
dried up
on the furniture in our old house.
In the middle of the night, you handed me your worn prayer beads.
Visit me in my dreams,
I am forsaken without your palm's henna,
aged and decrepit without your spirit
so visit me
in my dreams
Don't be afraid
I will conceal our reunion as best as I can.

SAADIA MUFARREH is a poet, critic, and writer who lives in Kuwait. A 1987 graduate of Kuwait University with a degree in Arabic language and education, she has published four collections of poetry, including *He Was the Last of the Dreamers* (1990), *When You're Absent, I Saddle My Suspicion's Horses* (1994), *Book of Sins* (1997), and *Mere: A Mirror Lying Back* (1999). She is a regular contributor to several Arabic newspapers and magazines and serves as art editor of the newspaper *Al-Qabas* in Kuwait.

REFRIGERATOR

Translated by Nay Hannawi

I opened it.
Its contents were tidy.
Bottles of preserved milk,
cartons of yogurt,
bags of frozen meat,
yellow apples,
medicine, bread
and . . . and . . . etc.
In the refrigerator of my soul
the contents scatter
and expire
and remain closed.

Loss

Translated by Nay Hannawi

On the side roads
I stroke my hair hidden by necessity.
I sneak my right hand into my pocket.
I walk like a swan.
I swing my bag in the new air.
I sing my spontaneous songs.

But the side roads are crowded,
And the swan doesn't know the language of ants.

SOON SHE WILL LEAVE
Translated by Hend Mubarek Aleidan, with Patty Paine

1
Soon she will leave. She is
busy choosing her finest dress.
She applies her make-up precisely,
and reviews missed calls
on her cell.

2
She is making an ordinary
lunch while writing her dead
poetry. She sings
with the rhythm

3
of the Gulf.
She mixes surprise
with wet salt, she draws her small
house of gray stones.

4
She creates language
and it dances
on arpeggios.

For who, all these words?
For who is she sharpening
her pencils?

5
With a touch she creates
humanity and its last days.
She needs no philosophy
to give existence reason.
She fills joy's halls
with secrets, she travels
to places with no maps.

6
She darkens her eyes
with kohl, draws on
her favorite lipstick,
then she leaves her room
full of crime.

DISTANCE

Translated by Nay Hannawi

Between the room and hall
is a corridor of broken tiles.
So small, my mother complains.

Only my aching body knows
how long it really is.

Salem Sayar Mohsin Al Anzi is currently working at the Ministry of Information in Kuwait. His poetry addresses the nation, the family, the oppression of women, and issues related to the Arab, Islamic, and global communities. He has participated in several poetry events and festivals in Kuwait, Oman, Egypt, and Jordan and at the American University in Al Shariqa, Kuwaiti ministries, and the Gulf University in Bahrain. He participated in "Towards a Better Space", a festival organized under the auspices of Her Highness Sheikha Mozah bint Nasser Al Missned, consort of the Emir of Qatar His Highness Sheikh Hamad bin Khalifa Al Thani. He was awarded the best poet distinction at the Festival of the Arab Poet and by *Deerah* and *Jeans Magazine*.

THE STORM

Translated by Camilo Gómez-Rivas

I must be,
more than yesterday, composed.
I must
make myself smart
from the first rib
to
the last of a lover's detail
and wear
        expressions of dismay
from the first sign
of departure
to the last sigh of absence,
from the day a parting appears
on the horizon.
        I folded into myself

and locked the door of the question.
The night is possessed.
     Fatigue.
And not a drop of blame
in it.
Sad, she cries out wailing.
Tonight I dress in wishes
and songs
drape leaves on my wounds,
     a forceful dispossession.
Were I depressed
I would say:
I am not sad, and depressed.

It is written:
     And the one who will be
no doubt will be.
God is generous.
This I have known:
     hearts
always arrive at odds
     as do men
in their heads,
     But their temperament
unites them.
I have decided, inevitably,
to be,
even with the separation,
     composed,
with a rib belt
over
my heart, and will make myself patient
and be
always composed of affection.
The night, I know,

will pass,
within my head
like a storm.

BUNDLE OF WOUNDS
Translated by Camilo Gómez-Rivas

Tonight they are a bundle of wounds and papers
and I am dispersed to the end of the night and I stay
with nothing to do but ignite all the sighs of longing.
Burning tears are what remains of the longing
and what I say constricts the chest, but when it tightens
my ribs break over my soul and I am miserable.
Alone my eyes fill, prominent and departing.
Crying was separation behind tears of separation.
Good then! Take me to the people by embrace
and this time, it's just you and me. Good then. We will stay.
Is it possible they didn't glide over the sea of stares
and didn't see my tears of longing?
This is me, from a night ago, standing and longing.
These are my palms of painful agitation, always drowning,
from night and sunrise to night and sunrise
and I return and repeat the story of the night, and I rise,
and I rise waiting for the night, star filled, while it rises.
I accompany it until the sky turns blue
and I remain alone and have nothing but these papers.
I write my wounds on them and remain.

A MISERABLE CHILDHOOD
Translated by William M. Hutchins

Pick yourself up,
Up, up!
Don't look for
Another person's hand
To comfort or raise you.
A loving heart is all you need.
Your siblings' and your mother's hearts
    Wait expectantly, throb, and travel
In fearful anxiety for your welfare;
Parents sweat to provide for you,
And their toil teaches you patience.
A single hair separates hopes from illusions.
Banish your illusions
And prove yourself.
Don't look around;
The rich don't know you exist
Nor do your princes.
They just hire you
To blister your hands,
Applauding and
Whistling appreciatively
For their poems at soirées,
Or to ride their she-camel
In the races.
From sorrows weave radiance
And fashion a homeland for your face.
Don't fret about all this;
You can achieve a lot
If you keep your head high.
You're the child most likely to succeed,

Grasping the life before you,
And the source of your lofty ambition
Lies in your right hand.

SHUROOQ AMIN was born in Kuwait in 1967 to a Kuwaiti father and a Syrian mother. She holds a Master's degree in English Literature from Kent University, UK and a PhD in Creative Writing from Warnborough University, UK. She is a poet, an artist, an interior decorator, a lecturer, and the head of the English Language Unit at the College of Business Administration, Kuwait University. Her poems and short stories have appeared in various literary journals, including *Diode*, *Etchings*, *Beauty / Truth: A Journal of Ekphrastic Poetry*, and *Words-Myth: A Quarterly Poetry Journal*. She published her first collection of poetry, *Kuwaiti Butterfly Unveiled*, in 1994.

ANOTHER DAY OF *EID*

Another day of *Eid*, and here is Yasmin with her
wedge-heeled, chinchilla-lined Manolo Blahniks,
her low-slung jeans in this season's sandblasted
shade, pot-glazed eyes smoldering with Arabic
kohl, exuding an air of sacrilegious opulence;

there goes politically-correct Salwa, in knee-
socks and nautical tops, utilitarian, unadorned,
loop-thin, invisibly hooked up to an intravenous
drip, being propelled by a dauntless stepmother
towards the made-to-order date-scones;

oudh-drenched Dana with her quick-setting-
as-concrete foundation, green frosted-glass
contact lenses, Cher-like hair extensions, and
Dolly Parton cleavage scoffs at Salwa
(who has succumbed to the scones, knowing

121

it's only a matter of minutes before she throws
them up into the guest toilet basin) and billows
ostentatiously across the room in eggplant-brown
mock-couture, coordinated accessories clinking
like aural winking.

Little Lina with her corkscrew hair (done at Jacques
Dessange at the last minute) lifts her softly-tiered,
polka-dotted tulle dress to sit down next to her mother,
tries to itch an arm through manifold layers of softly
gathered chiffon—but can't; cries silently in frustration.

Like a sun-suffused freak in a Diane Arbus photograph,
I mingle amongst the family, as translucent as a
sea-gooseberry. My patience thickens like gouache
when I catch sight of my bespectacled, aqueous self
in an ornate mirror. I feel queasily androgynous.

Time slithers slow as a lugworm, roils around
my aura, chokes me with musk and ambergris,
marabou capes and cashmere ponchos;
a plethora of millefleurs and chintz
generates sparks and static all around me.

As I sink into my own geek-infested waters,
I glance at my watch, counting the hours
until I'm back in that villa by the sea, sipping
Amaretto and smoking cigars after sex, back
to my wax-sealed affair with Yasmin's husband.

FATE OF THE GULF MARINER

Garlic-pink,
blue-swirled sky
regurgitates
seasons for

me to course
through clove-black
seas, lateen
sailed; myrrh burns

evil eye;
shark-oil sealed
planks stitched with
palm-husk threads;

emerald
whorls, flute-like,
play for dill-
fish; my skin

catches kale-
green, digs gold
runnels for
four months of

spring on my
sambouk; I
catch them lit
mottled in

gill-nets, pearls
and fish to
live; and you,
my son, hair

sea-sticky
like palm-leaf
matting, brown-
leather skin

thin from years
of diving,
breath borrowed
by waves that

slurp the shore,
tell me, son,
as you lie
heartbeat-less

on my deck,
how to spare
your mother
these tidings.

OLFACTORY BAZAAR

The cardamom pods have been drying
for days on old stiff newspapers
in kitchens wafting saffron breezes;

the effluvium of *tanoor*-baked *saj* bread
drifts past the perfume of old *bukhoor*
sticks petering out near the window sill,

and crinkled men with nutmeg-flecked
skin carry on smoking grape *shisha*, its
whiffs whisking through this forties-café,

infiltrating blocks of fused blue sky
and scraggily tangential red-sand dunes;
turmeric roofs reek trendy store-bought

eau-de-toilette, glossy in its French packaging,
drifting past the pong of Indian incense on
the marble-topped kitchen table, out of open

double-glazed windows trailing the stench
of depression and another life about to end
itself in today's new crisp newspaper.

POETS FROM OMAN

The Sultanate of Oman lies in the southeast corner of the Arabian peninsula, facing the Arabian Sea and the Gulf of Oman and bordering the United Arab Emirates, Saudi Arabia, and Yemen. It has a population of just under three million, about twenty percent of whom are expatriates and guest workers. Although it has close and longstanding ties with Great Britain, it has never been a British colony. Today it is ruled by the Al-Said family, advised by the popularly elected Majlis Oman. For centuries it has been a center for trade, but more recently its income has come from oil, natural gas, and tourism. With dwindling oil reserves, however, in recent years the government has placed a priority on expanding educational opportunities and research in the areas of agriculture, minerals, water resources, and marine sciences.

SAIF AL RAHBI is a poet and writer born in 1956 in Sroor, a village in the interior of Oman. Beginning in 1970, he traveled extensively abroad, studying journalism in Cairo and living and working in Damascus, Algeria, Paris, London, and other Arab and European cities. He is the editor-in-chief of *Nizwa*, Oman's quarterly cultural magazine. He has published a number of volumes of poetry and prose and essays and is a consulting editor of *Banipal.*

DISTANT WATERS

Translated by Anton Shammas

In the murky mirrors of distant waters
the bird of desire soars beyond a sealed horizon
Faces split by the cawing of years
Chariots bark behind the walls
As if you came for a trip preceding birth
you follow a grand funeral of reminiscences
wearing a shirt stained with the blood of distances.

Struck with amnesia, camels
are lost in the alleyways
Dynasties crossing the desert
all drowned in quicksand
You walk with a lonely step
leaving every place its private wound
and every minaret a belt of howls.

Body smeared with departures,
those who came from distant waters tell you to stop
and watch your sin fleeing.

ARRIVAL
Translated by Abdulla Al-Harrasi

When I travel to a country
rumors arrive before me
I feel intoxicated
like a wolf whose dreams beat him to the prey
So I don't arrive.

BELLS WILL NOT TOLL TONIGHT
Translated by Abdulla Al-Harrasi

The storm in front of my door
will not subside tonight.
Its Herculean armies have slammed shut the doors.

In the church's fading light
I glance at monks pulling handcarts,
fleeing to the mountains
on horses that stretch and strain into the wind
as if from the Byzantine age.

On this memorial night
bells will not toll,
the storm will never subside.

FRIENDS

From the dreariness of the road
they came
bundled up in coats whose belts
were the autumn of water-springs.

Their wounds galloped over
mountains and dreams
but never made it.

MUSEUM OF SHADOWS
Translated by Anton Shammas

White birds cross wide rivers
on nights more lonesome than widows of war.

Bridges and closed-eyes trees strolling
with passers-by,
as if in a museum of shadows.

From a distance you could see their shadows, staggering
among the stupidity of daytime's
empty bottles.

You know them, one by one—
incurable curse,
nameless glories.

They came from a house next to your dreams,
searching for a heart more merciful than knowledge
and under the enormous shadows of a somber dawn
they all disappeared
except for a single peal of laughter.

NO COUNTRY WE HEADED TO
Translated by Anton Shammas

No woman we loved
the enemy didn't conquer first.

No country we headed to
fire didn't level down to the ground.

No wound we bandaged with our eyelids
didn't fling wide open.

No arena
No child we begat under horses hooves
(What horses?)
No horizon, or memory unbuttoning
in the splendor of its hallway.

No childhood, even remote like Saturn
No lion, as he left at dawn along with his lair
The mountains' eternal foundations collapsed
I don't hear the crows cawing in the arac trees
Eagles were hanged by summits
No echoes
Nothing at all.

Our Old House
Translated by Abdulla Al-Harrasi

White clouds wrap the neighboring sky,
and accompany travelers to their distant villages.
And we are swimming in the festival rain,
where birds gently pecked the air,
to wake it, with us, on the roofs,
where we dried our dates and dreams
on the clay balconies
and fell between the feet of an agitated bull,
where the stains of an enervated sun
seized the house, with its birds and women
and ancient trees stumbling like
shepherds among ruins.

Beyond the fence
you can still see the palm trees,
like bewildered spirits colliding with minarets,
like ships lowering their sails
in misty seas,
and amid their somnolence and green dreams
lurks the evening's next soirée.

SCREAM

Translated by Anton Shammas

The scream that's sunk inside
like an animal buried in a cave, prowls around
sleepers, along with its foreign soldiers,
forces them to go to
uncharted, distant lands.
The scream that comes down from the age
of enormous floods – my only
travel guide
my spoiled woman whom sometimes
I watch duping hyenas in my bed
then falling asleep in my etherized, tranquil
arms.

At times it falls upon distant summits,
wailing, like a primordial widow.

But tonight, as she abandons me,
I see at the far end of the forest
a wounded tigress watching me in admiration.

Suitcase

A man lives in a suitcase
his feet are crossroads—
a gloomy sky at each.

Once he saw a flock of sheep on the horizon
and remembered his grandfather
He lit a candle inside a cave
and kept circling it
century after century
until his shadow cracked
and his days welled up with tears.

A TRAMP DREAMING OF NOTHING
Translated by Anton Shammas

And like a wave clawing
a hurricane,
I entered this world's wilderness
throwing the treasures of my forefathers to the bottom of hell
honing my limbs on an exile-forged
blade.

And like a child who's always losing the game,
I didn't expect much from my ilk
I didn't expect anything
but the clamor of doors and windows
being opened and shut near my head
with the innocence of aimless
storms.

But I exist and don't exist
knowing I'm hallowed with emptiness
A chronicle missing no detail
lit with magical lanterns
and you need to plough its
heart for a
single tear
or confession.

You need to follow the moon of departure,
stretched between water and land, land
and grave,
in order to see a shadow in a cave.

A genie trembling in awe of God,
napping on the devil's
thigh.
But I am here . . . Maybe now
I'm in a café,
watching the world from behind the glass
The pale sunset,
a hangover after yesterday's trip
I'll extinguish with today's
and not care about anything
Let rivers dump their cities of garbage
into the sea
Let vagrants spit at the shrines of saints
and soldiers crop the heads of their barracks,
Let eagles soar high or low
That's all.

It would be redundant to discuss
the relation between mouth and spring
or a village delirious under
the trap of the flood's ribs,
or nice evenings of poets who dream of suicide aboard
a boat slowly sinking into water's
haze
or by an axe suddenly plunging,
with no mercy.

You need to sell the furniture in your house
for morning coffee
(what house have you had?)
except for a tattered shoe over which
city nights stumble
and rags bequeathed to you by a dead friend
You remember (how could you forget?)
being chased by the scarecrow of poverty and Pharisees
and jackals

in Cairo and Damascus, in Beirut
and Algiers and Sophia and Paris and the rest
You remember it all, with the brilliance of birth,
the clarity of a crab crawling between
rivers like a tourist enchanted by Bedouin
tents.

O mother, sleeping on the bare
concrete
among the wreckage of hessian and scattered clothes
like the ruins of a village
razed by a thunderbolt.
There's no field left for your anticipating
visions
We no longer listen to the crowing of roosters
or bring fish from the beach
There's no dawn left whose feathers you play with
at the edge of the well
where you bade me farewell for the first time
seventeen years ago
(Don't stay away for too long!)
A single step blew up the orbit
of miles
and joined in the delirium of galaxies.

UNDER THE ROOFS OF MORNING
Translated by Anton Shammas

My scream is still blossoming under
the roofs of morning.
Your city couldn't stifle it.
My scream, on whose frost
I built a lawn—
a blind plunderer of the legacy of silence.
The screams of shepherds when their herd is startled
by a predatory animal
The screams of saints and demons
at the edge of doomsday
She carried it from town to town
like a nursing mother carries her child
like a tribe carries its seeds of origin
My only guide to the source of the river
in the blind darkness
in times of forgetfulness—
my scream under the roofs of morning
and night
is the witness to my silence
the witness of madness and pleasure.
You can't take that away from me
no matter how big the claws and weapons.

WATER BLESSED BY PROPHETS
Translated by Anton Shammas

Spoils granted by heaven
Water blessed by prophets
at the rock of their racking thirst
Flutter of the hoopoe's wing at Solomon's throne
From pain and delight you cry my love
from desire, erupting at the curve of longing

(My body's veins are hidden rivers)

You walk around stripped of a wedding ring on
your finger
You were the lake dreamt of by the winds.

You shut all doors
so I can open up a door or window
and look through at your dark cave
your concealed treasures
where crescents and baskets dangle
with ripe fruits
and gazelles through whose movements the ignorance
of those who passed before me seeps.
The luxurious find
for the body that's molded with a breeze
And for him who loiters in the night of organs
the blood of desire oozes
in search of the spring that flows with abandon
in the delirium of the forest.

ABUDULLAH AL RYAMI was born in 1965 and has been both blacklisted and arrested in Oman for his support of civil rights and his criticism of the government. He is co-founder of the avant-garde theater group A'Shams, where he works as dramatist and artistic director, and of Najma Publications, which specializes in modern poetry, novels, and works in translation. His first collection of poems was published in 1992.

PLEASE DON'T GIVE BIRTH!

Translated by Sarah Maguire, with Nariman Youssef,
Anna Murison, and Hafiz Kheir

No one predicted
the day I was born:
the breast that fed me
was a jug of amnesia spilt by the invaders.
So I throw myself onto my shadow
to save it from the approaching train;
I bare my chest to spears
as if I were a shield carried by my ancestors;
I climb mountain peaks
the way I stroll along the beach,
as if these mountains were my seas,
their caves my seashells, my days.
Now every tree hides a wall
beneath its bark:
the minute I touch it,
I trespass into the property of strangers;
the minute I sit down on a rock,
it sprouts wings and flies off.
Where can I go?

How can I stumble away
when I hang here like the plait
that splits my lover's back in two?
when God's name lashes from the minarets
like whips whipping horseflesh?
No one predicted the day of my birth.
And the river that bore me
has gone to ground
in a yawning expanse of endless
land that I cross without wings.
Like water, when I evaporate, I soar.
Like water, when I fall, I am pure.
Every time I touch this land,
its belly swells:
please don't give birth to another Omani,
an Omani who asks me
how long this century has lasted,
an Omani who invites me to his revels
to drink obedience in a cup–
while a rudderless balloon,
like an exclamation, floats across the sky.

SPEED

Translated by the Poetry Translation Centre Workshop, with Anna Murison

I take things lightly
that perhaps are heavy.
For example, I know I'm the gap between two sidewalks,
yet I cross it as fast as I can – why?
And because I take risks with my voice,
I trip on air.
And the first bead of sweat that trickles down my forehead
drowns me.
I take things lightly
that I know to be heavy.
This is the truth.
Yet I am nothing but an illusion—
a lantern
lost in a forest.
And whoever comes across these words
will find a large stone.
You can easily
throw it in my face.

GHALYA AL SAID is a poet and writer from Oman, living and working in London. She completed her secondary education in England, and earned a doctorate in international relations from Warwick University. She writes poetry in both English and Arabic and has published three novels in Arabic: *Ayam Fil Jena* (2005), *Sabra W'Assilah* (2007), and *Sineen Mubathara* (2008). She has participated in various conferences at SOAS (School of Oriental and African Studies), London and at Leeds University, where she contributed to *The Arab Diaspora: Voices of an Anguished Scream* (Routledge, 2006). She is also a member of Chatham House, the Royal Institute of International Affairs. Her sketches are used regularly in the independent pan-Arab daily newspaper *Al Quds Al-Arabi* to illustrate poetry and short stories.

THE CAR

The open window
The quiet wind
The traveling night
(we can't move)
the static bus
the frozen, tired passers-by
all of frightened, gummed up London
and your eyes
saying goodbye.

Malika and the Zar Dance

Cave, mountain, streams of clothes
The discovery of her lifetime: take take, taken;
Keep keep, kept;
Fly fly, flown away with the dream.
Labels flutter everywhere, a sequence
Of beads, draped fabric
Names dripping – Issey Miyake, Comme des Garcons,
Yohji Yamamoto–
So many delicate expensive names
Floating away under Waterloo Bridge
Where she dances at night under the sky. She prances for all
these names.
They should be her friends, leave their ivory Bond Street towers
To share her ecstatic celebration.
But all that appear are a fragrant
vagrant or two, her night friends thrilled by her dancing.

She dances while the river drifts away
The seagulls above her scream their nightly raptures
And she jumps over empty bottles and cans,
Still dancing,
the vagrants encouraging her
"Go on girl, higher, more, go for it!"
Til the dance turns sublime, a Zar dance
Where dreams and fantasies mingle in a different world
And all those exclusive labels become people.

Now she can have them as friends–
But at the end of the dance all she finds is her own
Disheveled body
Lying in the cold under Waterloo Bridge

Somewhere a train clattering through the distance
Carrying nothing
Except the emptiness of her night.

MOHAMED AL-HARTHY was born in al-Mudhayrib, Oman in 1962, and has a degree in geology and marine sciences. He is the author of four poetry collections: *Ouyoun Tewala al-Nahar* (1992), *All Overnight* (1994), *Farther than Zanzibar* (1997), and *Luba'h la Tumall* (2005). In 2003, his book *Ayn wa Janah* won the Ibn Battuta Prize for geographical literature. His travel book *Ouyoun Tewala al-Nahar* (2004) chronicles his visits to the Virgin Islands, Zanzibar, Thailand, Vietnam, Andalusia, and Saudi Arabia's Empty Quarter. He has participated in several poetry forums, festivals, and workshops in Cairo, Jordan, Morocco, France, and Germany.

A LITTLE BEFORE REACHING DEATH

Translated by Camilo Gómez-Rivas

This is a story I left on the grass, on the grass under the tree,
and I returned to carry on my back,
its sins – or mine. Which?
I don't know.

I returned not knowing, so I left it there on the grass,
stripping the night of its utter darkness, dragging
the night toward the whitened wave (from pain perhaps)
or perhaps from joy
a little before reaching death.

Again, I do not know, forgetting a story
I left on the grass, and I don't know
        whether its sins or mine are on my back.

APOLOGY TO THE DAWN

Translated by Camilo Gómez-Rivas

In detail undesirable in the craft of poetry,
⠀⠀⠀⠀⠀I like to mention the times of day in verse,
such as day and night, morning and evening,
noon and what follows . . .

⠀⠀⠀⠀⠀But I always forget the dawn.
Just as I forget that I am burdened with the stone of Sisyphus
(worn from so much rolling in books).
⠀⠀⠀⠀⠀I forget it, regrettably, in spite of its being my guide
to life before waking, my key
to the gist of more than one poem, in the heart of the stone,
where sparrows wake on the window sill,
migrating with their voices from branch to branch
as if from one continent to another, from branch
to branch between one recital and the next,
in the heart of the stone, they tell me,
(as I return from the kitchen with a glass of tea)
flying in the air, from on top of a branch,
or pecking grain on the window sill:

"Quit that piano concerto
and apologize to the dawn with a poem.
We will shower you with music and inspire you with rhyme."

PAWNS OF SAND
Translated by Sargon Boulus

The drowned remained
in their bottled dimness
and the moon drifted
on its course.
The ironed djellabas
also kept waiting
for their lives
which the hunt
had taken to a gathering
dusty with preys.
And the crow
  who with his eyes
had bled a feather
  that neglected
to place a horse
  in the grassy landscape
couldn't find
  a new trick
for landing on trees
or even just a color
that can still muffle
  the sound of
  falling leaves
in a hall filled
  with shadows.

No one came
  to their aid

They didn't exchange
the half-words
with which to wet
    the camels' glances
and nothing else
    happened as
    well.

Because
    they just
waited for all
    that time
until they were dead.

At a Slant Angle
Translated by Sargon Boulus

You were not
the meanings' cohort
or its opposite,
but between two doors
you paced with half-words,
you scaled the roof of dream
with the fabled
adventure, stalked the arm
and cane that became
a road, as evening fell
in the elegies and
the mirrors.

Nor were you alone
as you went down the slope
of your life where
you weren't alone.
your hand lit the candles
of air, the dawn's photograph
wove the morning haze
with a sleepy needle
and a morningless woman's
        lock of hair
in the immense mirror
that reflects the same image
with a slanting angle
        at the end of the slope
you never understood
        was your life
                itself

hung at the entrance
       to paradise.

REEM AL LAWATI of Oman began writing poetry at the age of fifteen under a pen name. She used a pen name because her poetry often deals with relationships and topics of love and romance which are sometimes considered taboo. Her latest collection of poetry is *Invented Stupidities* (2006).

THE CHRONOLOGY OF WATER
Translated by Ghada Gherwash

Like a prophecy
Knocking on the door
A nearby scent does not shut its lids except with a sip that observes
The horizon with astonishment
This bar resembles the nostalgia embodied in the dregs of a glass!

A Mistake

A glass of water
Is it like a glass of wine that flows from an embrace?
Or perhaps a spray in the darkness of the clouds
As vast as the sky

Arid

Every time absence comes close to silence
The time for drunkenness departs

A Crazy Man

What a message this being has
And what a wise narrative;
He believes more strongly in the prophecy than in himself
From God's water to Eve's clay.

Loins

Before he disgraced the secret
His sins surrounded him
And his short hand touched the edge of fear;
He prayed awkwardly!
He did not know how to be a celibate
Maybe he was born with the sting of salt
In a brothel that makes labor sting;
His worthless heart,
His mother,
What's left of the prophecy is wandering in the streets
Looking for a lineage
For this night!

MAY LOVE BE PRAISED
Translated by Issa J. Boullata

About him:
    Praise be to Him who has made love a "fate" for us
    Offer your rose before the dream is extinguished
    This month is one of God's months that is beginning
    O strange woman
    And the farthest distance from you is alienation

About her:
    Praise be to Him who has made a "fate" for us
    of one love meeting another love
    and who has made Time more knowledgeable than we are
    Two eyes observing the horizon of love's absence, wondering
    will it rise when the sunrise is on the wane

Both singing:
    Have mercy on a love that is more
    than a woman coming out of a man's rib
    more than a swelling, leaving an emptiness inside her
    Praise be to you
    she is the resurrection of a voice coming from non-being
    after life has flowed into its limbs

She/He:
    Primordial matter of chaos
    is what knocked on heaven's doors
    a kiss of intercession pouring out on its palms
    when night is more than a long chapter in the novel of time

He:

>Come, I will paint a star on your palm
>and the henna of vision on your other palm
>Wave to a direction no one knows but you
>and no one will tread on but me
>Make the dry river in my land gush
>There is water here that used to overflow
>being a flood of the gods of love

She:

>And washing myself in you
>is a bridge that God has extended between two hearts
>The water was abundant when it met us
>so abundant that it was drowned by us

Confidential whisper:

>This breath coming out from deep inside, "Aaah
>praise be to you. Help, help. Save us from yearning."

THE PSALMS OF LONELINESS
Translated by Ghada Gherwash

He roars alone;
A bubble emerges from the dream;
It left its message in the crazy kiss
He waves in the wasteland
Leaning on intoxication, a pomegranate!

Intimate
Leaping feverishly
To the imagination
Like foam whose waist an embrace hugs;
She has a sky
That reveals a honeycomb

Everything is open-ended
His goal is the flower
And her specialty is barren!

Holding the burning ember,
And in the man's fingers the viscosity of the human being
Creation
Even her mouth that's full of spilled
Temptations

Her spilled voice gurgles his presence
Rising like a pyramid that swings over history
In a resurrection
With a never ending descent!
Chamomile lurking in the body's suffering
Without fragrance
Isn't devoid of water that embraces the downpour!

An obtuse angle, on the triangle of celebration,
A party,
She exaggerated in beautifying herself for the future
                                    Chaos
And history conquers cities that lock up flowers,
A falling leaf
A bus in a strange land!

ZAHIR AL-GHAFRI was born in 1956 in Oman and is part of the avant-garde prose poetry movement. He studied in Baghdad and Rabat, and in 1982 earned a BA in Philosophy. He has published several volumes of poetry, including *Athlaf Baidaa* (1984); *Assamtu Ya'tee lel-i'teraaf* (1991); *Uzla tafeedu ani al-layli* (1993); *Azhar fee bi'ar* (2000); *Thilal be-lawni al-Miyah* (2006); *Kullama Thahara fe Malaki al-Qalaa* (2008); and *Hayat Wahida lakinna Assalalim Katheera* (forthcoming). Although he has lived in Iraq, Morocco, France, the US, and Sweden for extended periods, he currently lives in Oman and serves as the editor-in-chief of *Alberwaz*, a visual arts quarterly.

THE ANGEL OF POWER

Translated by Salih J. Altoma

We sit on the bank of this river
We, the prisoners of defeats, sit
waiting for the angel of power
to appear any moment now
radiating rage

Our voices are lost in distant orbits
There's no guide to lead us from the interminable waiting
behind doors, ignored by the winds

And so we wait
until the seven pillars of heaven turn white
Perhaps one day, on a day like this,
our wish will come, borne on wings
that glint like knives
and perhaps the sky will be filled with stars.

A ROOM AT THE END OF THE WORLD
Translated by Salih J. Altoma

In a distant room, at the end of the world
at the end of a stormy night
I remember you now as a phantom
accidentally passing near the fountain of my life
like a feather blown backwards
onto a land I rarely visit

I listen to your absence at the window of truth
The guests are gone
There's no trace of living shadows
nor flowers, either, left on the doorstep

My glance toward you while you are absent
is the repentance of the unfaithful
The sands scatter my dreams on your bed
and remorse perfumes you with the fragrance of water, white like the night,

You and I are two banks between which my life
passes as it floats on the glow of eternity
Tonight your fruits are golden
and music starts to play, a soft drizzle
from a distant room at the end of the world

THOSE YEARS
Translated by Salih J. Altoma

At times, I leave my life there with my comrades-in-pain
at the high walls of fate and walk on calmly,
a man wandering through an orchard
filled with scents of the past
I think I see, whenever I sit on river banks,
a smile forged from the flare of night

My dreams too, wave after wave of them, billow over the grass,
gleaming like pure gold.
I live in a city that meanders through my memory. My father
guards time in deserted gardens. And my mother
gathers wood in the wilderness.
My life, in those years, was a journey
bearing only grapes of loss.
But in spite of that I knew
how to climb fortresses in the midday heat of the sun.

POETS FROM QATAR

Located on a small peninsula on the northeast coast of the Arabian peninsula, the State of Qatar borders Saudi Arabia. It has a fast-growing population of about 1.3 million, the majority of whom are expatriate workers from South Asia and from other Arab countries. It achieved its independence from Great Britain in 1971 and functions as an emirate ruled by the Al-Thani family and by the popularly elected Majlis al-Shura. Although for centuries the area's economy was based primarily on pearling, today its primary source of income is oil and natural gas. Though late among the Gulf states to develop, since the 1990s Qatar has become a leader in the areas of higher education and research.

SOAD AL KUWARI was born in Doha and graduated from Qatar University. She works in the Ministry of Culture, Arts, and Heritage, supervising cultural events and the cultural salon of the Ministry of Culture, Arts, and Heritage. She has published five poetry collections: *Lam Takun Rouhi* (2000), *Wareethat al-Sahraa* (2001), *Bahtan ani al-Omr* (2001), *Bab Jadeed li-Dukhoul* (2001), and *Malikat al-Jibal* (2004). Her work has appeared in many Arabic and local newspapers and in several anthologies, including *Language for a New Century: Contemporary Poetry from the Middle East, Asia, and Beyond* (Norton, 2008). Al Kuwari has participated in events such as the Doha Cultural Festival and the al-Begrawiya Festival, Sudan and in poetry festivals in the UAE, France, Yemen, Switzerland, and Colombia.

THE FLOOD

Translated by Fatima Mostafawi, with Patty Paine

To murder freedom
we don't need generals,
or cannons. We don't need
weapons of mass destruction,
or podiums.

Erect a dictator's statue
in the middle of a crowded square
and watch
the pigeons fall
one by one.
Look how wisdom wears
the hat of obedience.

Cℛ❍

Coffee shops are havens
for intellectuals
and the unemployed escaping
houses haunted by echoes.

Prisons are built
for those who oppose,
for those who step
over the line, or fly
outside the flock.

The city is governed
by tyrants, wars are waged
by devils. The earth, like a grinder,
never stops crushing.

From which alley can we escape?
We are not lab rats
or horses trained for battle.
We are not your last bid
for power.

Cℛ❍

The clouds are aloof
and impede our view.
The cinema closes
our imagination. Quietly,
let's reshape history
along its endless surfaces,
along its endless mountains.

Inscribed on the walls of cafés:
the science of atoms,
acronyms, long arguments
over lexicon, death
of the author and the francophone,
And there, the last word
on reviving democracy
from its deep sleep.

MODERNITY IN THE DESERT

Translated by Sara Al Qatami, with Patty Paine

We talk of many things we don't understand.
Modernity in the desert! The latest
joke in a world full of jokes.
But this is the desert,
where dust hovers in the air like butterflies
in a graveyard.
Where sand blankets everything–
acacia and palms, the tents
of Bedouins, even camels,
the ships of the dunes.

So little can grow in the desert.

Our palaces scream cutting-edge.
Our A/Cs hiss like snakes.
Cell phones! Cyber cafés!

But remember, the desert is a fox
dressed like a woman.

THE QUEEN OF THE MOUNTAINS
Translated by Said M. Shiyab, with Patty Paine

My hands are stirring the fragments,
The brooks are threatened by desert,
The balconies surround mirrors.
The sea is alive with luminous creatures,
The sea is alive with blank questions,
And with the tremor of the seasons.

What is the bee saying to the sunflower?
What is it whispering to the sun?
To the fire burning in the corner,
To your trees rooted in the heart,
To your moon split between streets
To the wings of vision and suspicion?

What does the sunlight imply?
Numbers/words/loose sentences/shouts/dates/names?

What does the sunlight imply?
The rivers hurtling violently?
Spears/arrows/sharp swords/violence?

What does the sunlight imply?
Heavy rain/poems fleeing anthologies/flaming hell/
foggy intervals/roaming air/vigilance?

❧

I obstruct the way of the turtles,
Turn them over
And paint around them
huge circles like the eyes of an owl.

I bury my feet in a puddle of oil.

I cover my eyes with my palms
Shielding myself from the heat of August.
I flounder between one distance and another
And crash in a vacuum.

❧

O, you, eyes looking upward at the highest
O, you, reckless hands.
The queen of the mountains recites her charms,
And then throws them in the whale's mouth.
At the end of the night,
She returns to her cave.

❧

A petrified tear in her eye,
A lump in her throat,
In her heart are fallen cities and wounds.
It is said a huge frog inhabited this place,
And here a dove built her nest.
At wood's edge
A bird fell and another bird flew.
Therefore, I went out
To trace the fable of cats,
And the idle talk of women draped in black.

169

I went following the steps of the myth
Seeking the lie called happiness.
I went out . . . I went out
Into the headless shadows and spotted deer.
I went out then wished I hadn't.

MARYAM AHMAD AL-SUBAIEY is a writer from Qatar. She graduated with a degree in political science from the UK, and at the moment is working toward her Master's in Development Studies, also in London. She works as political activist, has contributed numerous essays and articles in the Qatar Narrative Series, *Woman Today Magazine*, and is also a popular blogger. She works too as a junior editor in a publishing house in London, and has prepared and presented writing workshops in both Arabic and English. She is currently working on her first novel.

THE INVISIBLE ARMY

They wrap their dry faces with a dirty cloth.
If they're lucky they have a plastic helmet.

The sun squashes them like we squash a moth.
We leave them lying, burning until we collect
them at sunset.

They are canned in a bus,
then canned in their rooms.

Their expressions are wiped
by sun, dust, the law, and by us.

They try to run from the burning sun.
They try to erase the endless dust.
But there is nowhere to run to escape
the sun and dust.

Behind the dust all you can see
is their broken souls and the shine
of new cars mirrored in their eyes.

They are not as human as we are.
They are nothing
but workers. We don't want
them in our malls, we chose
not to see them, to forget them.

This army that builds our country
remains invisible beneath the burning sun.

DHABIYA KHAMIS studied political science and philosophy at Indiana University and the University of Washington in the US, and modern Arabic literature and anthropology at the University of London, UK, where she also edited the literary magazine *Awarq*. She received her Master's degree in Arabic Literature from the American University in Cairo. She has long been affiliated with the Arab League, being responsible for women and the family and for culture and serving as ambassador to India. Her poetry, prose, and literary criticism have been translated into German, Spanish, English, and French, and she has published over forty-five books of poetry, fiction, and Arabic translations.

DELHI'S GARDENS
Translated by Abir Zaki, with Patty Paine

I collected the light's dust
From the gardens of New Delhi

On an ancient rock
I etched scenes of the city
Like a Stone Age man
From memory chronicling history
Soft, and remote is this day
It sheds its skin like a snake
And flows from seasons to season
Water, fire and light . . .

I was grabbed by its ghosts
Between its palaces, tombs, and altars

Pierced by its lushness
And by the uncertainty of the unknown
I walk through gardens that masterfully conceal
Former ages

Incense, music, the gilded covers of books
And the statues of the Gods
Remain in my bosom today
Saying that this is Delhi . . .
Delhi, the profile of her face is
Hidden in the heavens.

THE HISTORY OF THAT TREE
Translated by Abir Zaki, with Patty Paine

⊙

Violence is the guillotine of History
blood is food for Power
skulls are the throne of Time.

Whoever bows in front of someone
facing the wind with a sorrowful expression
leaves blood at the gate of the conqueror.

Give me the freedom to say that
the forest with its Saints is etched on my neck.

No desire to disclose
for the fear of the "other" is my comrade
no lust for militancy
nor need to speak on behalf of "people"
nor to be thrown in the arms of comrades
just to be like them.

Give me a berry's leaf
so that I can cover my eyes and not see the flaws of history.

Give me a morphine injection, or a morsel of
hashish so that I forget all the lessons I've learned.

I take my breath empty handed
and with a broken wing like all Arab citizens.

I expose the day that was yesterday's graveyard
rebelling over its details
sloughing the slogans off my back
that overwhelmed me since my first moment
on this earth.

Nothing can force me to stand by,
and the law, in any case,
is not my law.

I scream in the face of the sun,
on the edge of my path
the mountains have no edges
the valleys are my asylum.
My Arabism is a cloak that can't disguise my loins
who like me are victims
falling like witch's dolls
armed with pins of death and disability.

I will address you in the space of history
why did you deceive me?
I am like a sparrow that goes to its trap
thinking it has wings that flap.

I steal my life from my death
I steal my freedom from my volcanic-tempered executioner.

I am defeated and afraid
like an autumn leaf that fell
followed by the fruitful tree it died upon.

And no one. No one
knows the history of that tree.

SCENTED WALLS

Translated by Abir Zaki, with Patty Paine

Within scented walls
the world seems larger.
It's so easy to press the button
to change the scene.

Instantly we can be
in the African bush, for example.
We can watch the lazy lion yawn, satiated,
instead of all these faces,
the ones known and unknown,
fallen, killed or murdered
in wars with no borders.

Under the warm cover
a cup of anise, or scented tea on the nightstand
you may read or leave
when you like.
You can reshape your life in this world
for there's Aphrodite,
the Iliad,
the Mutanabi, and Veda
the reminder to the son of David, and the apses of Ibn Arabi.

You may walk amongst souls
and befriend them,
in serenity you alone can be with them . . .

Over the lamenting
and crying
the brawling and commotion
in the street . . .

You can almost hear the psalms of David,
the music of the Sitar,
the carols,
and if you want you can dance to the pulsing
rhythm of the African drums.

Sky Rain

Translated by Abir Zaki, with Patty Paine

My beloved,
The sky will rain

All over again

What this might be:
The Pharaoh's Nile
In the beginning of its creation
While the breeze wets the spirit
in the flowing water
in its streams . . .

Where is the divine?
What leaps from the box into memory?

Do we see it?
It's as if we've never seen ourselves, ever . . .

ZAKIYYA MALALLAH was born in 1959 in Doha, Qatar. She received a PhD in Pharmaceutics from the College of Pharmacy, Cairo University in 1990. She is currently the head of quality control in the laboratory/ pharmacy department at the Ministry of Public Health in Qatar and a writer in the cultural section of the journal *Al watan*. Malallah is the author of nine books of poetry. She is a member of the League of Modern Literature (Egypt), the Ahram Cultural Club, the World Academy of Art and Culture (US), the World Poetry Academy (India), and the Women's Union (Paris). She has won many poetry prizes, participated in numerous radio and television programs, and given poetry readings worldwide. Her poetry has been translated into Spanish, Urdu, and Turkish.

LITTLE TALES
Translated by Wen Chin Ouyang

Flap your wings on my bare trees,
teach me
the little tales . . .

There once was a lady in love
who hid her bags
and fell asleep in the hair strands of noon.
She roamed my body,
bared herself in my soul
and fluttered her wings, a prisoner of my heart.
I housed her in my Gardens of Eden;
bitter poetry
trickled through her silent lips.

❧

I know her.
She came to me every evening, bearing her tremor,
her eyes sunk in the edges of the robe tied around her body,
her hands are oars,
wrestling with the waves of defeat in the bottom of her chest,
breathlessly,
left behind by the footsteps of destiny,
strewing around the passion she has been carrying between her teeth
and asking forgiveness between my hands.

❧

When she came to me
I was radiant,
my face almost glowing with the magnanimity of a prophet
and the blood of saints quivering in my eyes;
I became frightened,
apprehensive,
kindling my fire.
The smoke was circles of silence
and my burning was my lifeboat.

❧

She said: you have it so pure—
turns her face toward the cities,
gathers tulips,
pulls out thorns from palms,
brings green back to eyes,
unravels locks of desire.

❧

She said:
my awakenings are countless.

One
She comes when the horizon turns cloudy,
when the stars of slumber roam about,
when the moon shines
wearing a robe the color of wheat
and spilling roses,
leaning on a cane of light
while the dusk follows you,
parting the darkness to make a path for you.

Two
Your sky is filled with fragrance.
Your cloud
is a loaded scripture
that rained
seasons of shadows,
and sprouts of fertility and growth.

Three
You know me as a gypsy river,
washing in the sun's volcano,
bestowing the honor that is Isis on me.
Your doors are closed
and your walls silenced
but you slip away through a crack or cavern.

Four
Sleepless in your night,
aflame by your embers;
I emit fire
and the fire spits me out,

it chatters on your cloak,
getting undressed,
seeking cover in snow flurries.

Five
Acacia branches stretched in your limbs
and trees of pebble grew.

She quarreled with me and said,
"whether we make up or not,
I have made up my mind to leave, to go to a faraway place;
and going away will
douse the fire of passion;
and perhaps thorns will grow between fingers,
and sprout from bleeding lips."
So let us go our separate ways;
and between you and me, may a lifetime weave its web,
may a cloud hover.

And one day she came upon me:
"I will bid you farewell.
I have not risen to your heavens,
I have not tasted your evening.
May alienation prevail in your life,
may you not slip the fleeting moment from our cup!"
I twisted upon my trunk,
and curled my branches around me.
If only she had warned me,
I would have let warmth flow with the tears of my eyes
and she would have napped between my ribs,
like a rebellious cat, my rebellious cat.

IF YOU WERE MINE
Translated by Samia Touati

If you were mine
If this shadow were once our home
If flowers were every scent of us
and in our hearts, the shivering of affection
an endless truth
in my mind, I embrace
in my soul, I kiss
If you were mine
you are a winter cloud pouring down
a blossom that embraces lightness
a seagull racing the wind
If you were mine
you would be
a butterfly folding me in its wings
and cloaking me in its love
whenever I cried sorrowfully
immersed in longing
If you were mine
like a spring breeze
a shivering of string
a moon rising in the sky
hugging the stars, clouds and rain
If you were mine.

BLENDING

Translated by Samia Touati

A color
two
three
on the brush,
various paints blended
on the canvas,
a face is revealed
a pinched nose
parched lips
teeth swallowing teeth
was your face painted on mine
or am I two faces in your mirror?

OBSERVANCE
Translated by Samia Touati

I contemplate myself
like a horizon
approaching my heavens
I neither rise
nor set
I lean on a pitchfork
and pick up years of wheat.

ISOLATION
Translated by Samia Touati

I isolate myself
I remove my medals
I strip my skin from the king's peacock
I declare myself

ABDULLAH AL SALEM was born in Doha in 1975 and has also lived in Saudi Arabia, the UAE, and Jordan. In Qatar, he has served as manager of the Doha International Centre of Interfaith Dialog. On his website, www.wosom.net, he publishes his literary work, including poetry, literary criticism, short stories, articles, and letters. He holds a Master's degree in Law and is currently pursuing a PhD.

A CELEBRATION OF LOSS
Translated by Hart Uhl

A year.
Her scent in my clothes,
Her taste in my mouth.
When dawn is announced,
I hear the echoing of her laughter
Reverberating between the minaret and my footsteps.
A year.
One thousand coquettes interrupt my solitude.
They all defy death over my pliant corpse:
Loved ones, innocent relatives, chivalrous friends, traitors.
A year.
My anticipation for her was as always,
But now I know that her candles will burn out.
Darkness will consume the ends of my table.
I will weep alone, encountering no one.
This shattered boy will learn how stupid he is.
A year.
Time passes scornfully.
Seventy thousand died, but for what?
Seventy thousand died on the path.

Seventy thousand were destroyed at the entrance of the barracks.
And you are as you are.
The voice of life/the song of nature/turquoise/the grist mill,
wheat, and the smokestack.
A year.
I won't grapple with all her details;
She darts past my youth in vain.
I vacillate between "eternal truth" and "right guidance".
I pendulate between chivalry and poverty.
A year.
One thousand girls interrupt my solitude.
They defy death over my pliant corpse:
Loved ones, innocent relatives, chivalrous friends, and betrayers.
They expend all of their energy
For the impoverished/vagrants/laborers/and me
While I am left begging in the mean streets
For alms from her face.

DOWNTRODDEN PEOPLE
Translated by William M. Hutchins

୬

Downtrodden people,
Afflicted by fate with its worst punishments,
Don't wish for anything,
Don't desire anything.
. . . their brows are furrowed
And their spotless complexions turn sallow.
They abhor greed for petrol
In barren hills;
It's just a current fad.

Downtrodden people:
Youth's nectar flows pure for naught, and
Its naked clusters dangle.

Each bunch is available;
Just come,
Pull off as many as you want.
Apple, fig, and almond cascade down.
Every act is permissible;
Just come;
Slip your foot into any soft skin you like
For a paltry sum,
Of only a few dirhams.
Then rise and spit out:
You Beauty!

Downtrodden people:
Softer than a feather's fluff,
Gentler than a child's laugh,
Simpler than gushing water.

Debased people:
Remnants of an honorable life glisten in lackluster eyes.

In their valises,
Silently, with a smirk, they tote tragedies,
Concealing toys and gifts for their kids
Beneath cosmetic cases,
Beside letters from their family.

They are like us . . .

. . . .

. . . .

. . .

Downtrodden people:
Their sorrows seep
Into their tired blood.

. . .

Do you suppose
That if we awoke unexpectedly
One day
As downtrodden people,
We would spill as much blood
Into chalices of debasement and misery?
Or, would we remain just as we are
Scornful,
Respectable,
And honorable people?
All summer long our young men reserve
More than half of London
For dancing, drinking, snorting, cursing, and legendary generosity,
Giving our letter to others.
We're the most good-natured folks where money is concerned

And the most generous,
"And the generous man is merry."
Will we continue
To look down on other people,
Considering them flawed, cursed, stupid louts
Who shove their filth into our teaspoons, beneath our fingernails,
and inside our children's   copybooks,
Wantonly perpetrating their offenses in our streets?
Or, will we realize that it's wrong
To diagnose their ailments preemptively
From this vantage point?

EMERGENCY MEETING
Translated by William M. Hutchins

Baghdad, be patient. What's the rush?
We'll come solve the problem.
We've never forgotten you;
We've just been busy with related tales.
When we called an emergency
Meeting at a moment's notice,
We were caught off guard by God Almighty:
The date conflicted with Elephant's Day.
For your sake, we bore the brunt
And showed ourselves icons of self-sacrifice.
So we met, despite pressing concerns,
Abandoned the blithe world,
And convened the initial session harmoniously,
But quarreled over the opening prayer,
Because it was religious and might
Excite divisiveness.
We were forced to examine the fantasies that
Some people might nourish
And what others might use as
Propaganda, a rebellion, or a bomb.
For your sake, we bore the brunt
And showed ourselves icons of self-sacrifice.
Then some of us yielded to others;
So we surmounted our differences on this subject
And moved on, a few days later, to
Another issue that created a stir.
We had earmarked a reasonable sum
To cover our reasonable attack
But fell out over counting it: in
Pennies or raindrops?

For your sake we bore the brunt
And surmounted our differences on the subject.
Then we passed a revolutionary manifesto
Rejecting the military aggression and any attempt to justify it.
(When our enemies read this tract,
Their lands will react explosively.)
We differed, however, on a release date
And agreed not to release it.
Be patient, Baghdad, because we're a nation suffering
From grievous wounds.
We hadn't concluded our funeral
For a martyr assassins betrayed
When we were outraged that Mira had been excluded
From competition in future episodes.
This turn of events is of such questionable legality
That a separate session will be devoted to it.
Baghdad, we form a single body, and
Should any member object, we'll amputate it.
That's why in desolate corridors of the Diaspora
Severed members curse us.
So be very calm till they're dealt with
While we're obliged to look the other way.
Tomorrow, if history thinks ill of us,
We'll concoct some phony tale.
Be silent in a seemly way, Baghdad,
About shameful rituals of forced entry
And expose your massive privates to them
Along with other used goods.
If they need a theater for wickedness,
Kneel when the rabble rise.

POETS FROM SAUDI ARABIA

The Kingdom of Saudi Arabia covers an area of over two million square kilometers and has a population of over twenty-eight million, eighty per cent of whom are Saudi nationals. It is both the largest and the most populous of the Arabian Gulf countries. It is also the birthplace of Islam and of the Prophet Mohammed, the home of the holy cities of Mecca and Medina, and the destination for the *hajj*, the annual Islamic pilgrimage. Ruled since the early twentieth century by the Al Saud family, Saudi Arabia's primary source of income is its oil revenues. However, it has recently begun to diversify its economy, starting with the establishment of six "economic cities" in different regions of the country to promote economic development.

NIMAH ISMAIL NAWWAB is a Saudi Arabian poet descended from a long line of Makkan scholars. She is a writer, editor, poet, lecturer, and a pioneering youth and women's activist as well as a photographer. Her English essays and articles on Saudi society, customs, Islam, art, crafts, cuisine, and calligraphy have been published in Saudi Arabia and abroad. Her poetry has been translated into numerous languages, and has been included in various international anthologies, including *Side by Side: New Poems Inspired by Art from Around the World*, *Other Voices*, *The World Strand*, and *I Belong*. Her work has also been featured in various print, radio, and television documentaries, including *BBC World News*, *Newsweek International*, and numerous others. Her nomination as a Young Global leader has led to her continuing to incorporate poetry to build bridges between the East and West. Her first volume of poetry, *The Unfurling*, was published in 2004 by Selwa Press, California. She is currently working on two poetry manuscripts.

THE STREETS OF MAKKAH

The streets of Makkah,
Long bordered with tall, tall homes,
White-washed homes, wooden homes,
Built on every corner, mountain top, ridge,
On the valley floor of the sacred land.

Tall, tall homes,
Centuries old homes,
Studded with brown aged latticed windows,
Overlooking mysterious labyrinths, winding walkways,
Alleys echoing with the passage of sounds,
Voices of those long gone.

Voices of families, friends all known to one another,
Welcoming strangers from other lands,
Spending *sheeshah**-filled nights,
Quite nights, loud nights,
In the open on the *dakkah***,
Hours of tea drinking, hours of tales,
Brimming with told and untold stories,
Of past generations, present generations,
Held in the collective memory,
A memory retaining the glorious past,
Undeterred by the present.

*Sheeshah: a water pipe used by men and women.
**Dakkah: a raised bench.

THE LONGING

Freedom,
how her spirit
haunts
hooks
entices us all!

Freedom,
will the time come
for my ideas to roam
across this vast land's deserts,
through the caverns of the Empty Quarter?

For my voice to be sent forth
crying out in the stillness of a quiet people,
a voice among the voiceless?

For my thoughts, that hurl around
in a never ending spiral,
to mature, grow, and flourish
in a barren wasteland of shackled minds?

Will my spirit be set free—
to soar above the undulating palm fronds?
Will my essence and heart be unfettered,
forever
freed,
of man-made Thou Shall Nots?

BANISHMENT

I release you my beautiful, terrible fear
—Joy Harjo

1
I let you out,
Your rule is at an end,
I let you out,
With all that is in me,
Grief,
I let you go,
Pent up wrath,
Clawing at my heart,
Clenching my hands,
Running your despairing, devastating course,
Through throbbing veins.

I give you back,
To the oppressors,
Tyrants,
Soulless,
Callous of human decency,
Giddy with hysterical racism,
Puffed with blind arrogance,
Thriving on their mastery,
Stealing, raping, conquering,
The Arab world, African continent, Asian lands.

I let you out,
As the agony of generations
Birthed,
Matured,
Ingrown,

Stamp our collective memory,
Moaning mothers,
Massacred young innocents,
Shamed helpless males,
Weaved in and out of the centuries.

I turn you out,
Grief,
Out of my heart of hearts
Out of my soulful soul.
I let you out,
As women's tears join
Across lands, deserts, oceans
Rivers of suffering,
Gushing and flooding,
The tributaries of time and place.
I let you go, Grief,
So you can no longer hold me in thrall,
Keep me from restful sleep,
Smothering my dreams,
With a bleak, murky future for my loved ones.

2
I let you out,
Grief,
And pick up the mantle of joy,
Pulling its swirling warmth tightly,
Deeply drinking up bubbling pleasure,
Dancing and twirling
To the ecstatic, mighty music of human bonding,
Soothing,
Supporting,
Succoring me,
Bringing me peace, peace, peace, peace . . .

Oh, yes, Grief, listen well,
As the bloom of hope thrives,
Spreads its fine pollen,
Cultivating laughter,
Confidence to take you on.

As streaming, quickening hope enters my soul,
Courses through my blood,
Races through my heart,
Shines out of my eyes,
I let you go,
Shrieking, writhing in denial.

Trying and failing,
To survive in a barren land,
Banished from the light of day
Banished from the soothing dark of night.

Your rule at an end.

ARABIAN NIGHTS

When the call of the *hudud*,
Echoes through the palm fronds
Carrying in their mists,
Visions, memories:

Caravans of high spirited steads,
Crisscrossing the endless seas of sand,
Rushing through the oasis,
Free, yet under control.

Of women washing in the hot springs,
Sheltered in the evergreen palms,
Weaving baskets,
Cooking, sewing, scampering after the herds,
Of days filled with toil.

Visions, memories:
Cascading starlight,
Casting its mild light over campsites,
The moonlight's silver shadow
Illuminating bearded faces,
Young boys thumping their feet
To the wild desert drum beat
*Dana, ya dan dan**
Singing of the pearls in the far away gulf
Dana, ya dan dan

The warm cardamom scented breeze
Carrying the fresh coffee aroma,
Warming, sizzling in the golden hooked pots

To the young giggling girls
Shyly peeking from behind the partitioned tent walls.

Flames flickering in the pit
Wood slowly consumed, sparks flying,
Dancing to the strain: *dana, ya dan dan*.

The cry of the *hudud*
Sweeps through the quiet morning air,
To the dawn of a new century.

Visions, memories,
Blown away by the winds of change.

*The refrain *dana ya dan dan* is a popular one used in Gulf songs.

THE AMBUSH

He watched the old movie unfold
The headcovered man bashing his van into a building
Nodding his head: "Yes another one, they are terrorists"
The calm way he uttered those words
The look in his young eyes,
Made me ache.

For they had won,
Hands down they had won,
Ultimately they had won,
Their hollow victory turning the world upon itself.

Those demented fanatics have implanted the bitter seeds
Our young believing that terror is to stay
Their questioning self-identity constant
Their questioning elements of society a fact,
Could I really answer?
Did I even *want* to answer?
No justification, no excuse can wipe,
Needless deaths, destruction of innocents,
Not a single life lost could be justified.

The land turned into a big gated occupied territory
The once-peaceful kingdom rent with shootouts,
As the tolerance of our peaceful spiritual beliefs
Is hijacked, twisted, used.

Power-hungry zealots
Misguided by the need for vengeance,
Vengeance against perceived,
Unacceptable ways of life,

Those whose hearts have been wiped clean,
Clean of the basic tolerance for fellow man
A tolerance making the religion thrive,
A spirit attracting billions to the faith,
All dashed on the rocks
In the surging ravaging river of hatred for the other.

As the very essence of our faith now stands in danger
Of this ambush from within,
Turning back upon them,
Derailing their intentions
As their hate colors their vision of the truth
That we are all, all, all
Sons and daughters of Adam
That the three faiths, our stay, our guide
Are interlinked, bonded forever
Sealed by The One
To spread their message of peace for human kind.

ILLUSIONS AND REALITIES

Sweeping robes
touched by the savage wind
fan out behind their delicate frames
each entity
stands statute still
and the ocean crests caress their footsteps
forming imprints in the wet, sandy harbor

Their eyes scan the waves
foam-topped, whipped to a fierce froth
echoing the frothy, unending walls of the accepted
lives churned up, lives pulled down

The laden, hardened figures stir
as their hands pull wind-swept hair, wind-swept dreams
shoulders stiffen, pull back,
ready to take up a stance
against rampaging nature
against mandated norms

And the spirits of ancestors join in,
their voices, cries, histories
unearthed from the oceans of forgetfulness
onto shores of reality,
as the new era breaks the bonds of normalcy
and the generations join.

They come from whole homes, broken homes,
homes teeming with *bakhoor**, and broken down shacks
along cracked borders, against rough rocks
gazing out at nature unbound

The bonds of perceived lives fall
on scattered, shattered shells
beneath emboldened sure footfalls

The robes flutter and sweep forth
as the figures of past and present
breath in the scent of release

Bakhoor: frankincense.

FREEDOM WRITERS

The scribe's spirit lifts
scenting the perfume of promising openness
taking a deep breath of tangy freshness
freedom of speech hailed in surprised jubilation
when the hardened bands of taboos
break, seep through the hardened cracks
of centuries of cemented, walled up silence

A shredded canvas set aside
a new tapestry emerges
with new strokes of images, music, songs
of a nation reborn

Eons of timeless taboos,
Caged, iced passions
     let loose
as the posture of abiding patience
     dissolves
And bottled up minions of silence
feel the blessed rain wash away
    the raw
     suppressive residue,
of judgment,
inequality,
     intolerance

Reality bends
    and breaks apart
      in a shower of brilliant breathtaking
              horizons

ALI GHARAM ALLAH AL DOMAINI, known by the pseudonym Ali Al Domaini, was born in 1950 in the village of Mahdara in the Al Baha region of the southern Saudi Arabian city of Taif. He received his Bachelor's degree in Mechanical Engineering from King Fahd University of Petroleum and Minerals, Dhahran in 1974. Al Domaini worked as the head of the Cultural Department in the Association of Culture and Arts in Dammam in 1978–1979. His books include *Winds of Sites* (1987), *Blank Times* (1994), *With Their Wings They Ring Window Bells* (1999), and *As We Open the Door* (2008). He worked first for Aramco and then for the National Commercial Bank (Alahli) in Saudi Arabia until his retirement in 2004.

THE SIGNS

Translated by Laith al-Husain and Patricia Alanah Byrne

The Sign of Dust

Dust has its dwellings
And signs have their tribes
Should my sight be blinded
their beginnings will touch me.
A night in the lap of a pregnant woman
And I not the agent:
if a boy it be, then he is mine
And if she gives birth to
"an enchantress"
then it is hers.
A bunch of suitcases saturated with dust
Woman of cities, she in whose halls the daylight filters
Love's hammock swings down here, rises there, so neither is water

drunk from its embers
nor voice borrowed from its silence
A horizon of hands the color of Turkish coffee,
Tatar in form
A rose of iron
Another of palm leaves
A third one unyielding . . .
So you who are about to rise up from the moss over the grave
How do you mend up the emptiness
And heal the wound of young maidens
And repair the vessels disintegrating on death's tracks.

The Sign of the Crayfish

I chose not to fight the enchantress of my youth against her wishes
and volunteered to rest
near the wall of wounded words.
I repented from resisting a song
which violates the dew
and gives license to
rain, to the branches of the
branches of the winds.
I chose not to teach my child that creation is of two kinds:
Woman and man
Man and woman.
Lineages of wine imbibed by creation
beam with signs
so gardens moan from the weight of bracelets.
I chose not to speak until I saw
Cities within villages
Coffins of silver taken and not bought
I chose not to see that which should be seen.
In the dream of one doleful from indiscretion
In the un-avowed pain between two intimates
I gave up trying to prevent my love from crying out:

only what is right, is permissible
in a time when the storm has forewarned of war!

The Sign of the Virgin
The carnation of morning said to its neighbor:
Master of the age of foliage
give me the rope, the cane and the harnessed wine jars
To ascend the horizon however difficult,
go up its ladder,
I, tree of love, am the flute's marked wind
turned part star, part medal
turn me into a young maiden and recreate me
Time has made room for the cloak of the dead
My own cloak is not soiled
I mend its braids across the horse's halter,
meet mariners
The country throws the talisman of
festivals into my lap,
I suckle it
And set it free
And in its birth refuse my death.

The Sign of Children
Morning's silence hung its lantern over the arch of the city
But I do not pass
I and the dust
And a glass of mud I fermented for two nights
Beautified with the yellowing of trees
We share this time its melancholies
And console the stone.
As evening approaches
And a woman who does not smile appears
Children in their beds sleep between notebooks and ink

Waiting for the paling of Thursday and the face of "news"
the dust and I fought over the waves
I let it go so it can depart
And depart so it can diminish
But it settles over my fruit!

A First dance
Artery of cities
You have bargained with me
With the metal loaf
And the milk of slumber
So drink blood now
To your fill.

The Sign of Eve
A portrait on the wall, gathering her jewels, tempts me
away from autumn's supper
I protect half of her with my shirt,
her loosening veil burns me
an Eden, eyes lined with tormented sweetness, its colors
drawn from a familiar time
How do I set up her crown in the vessel of dust, how?
I choose her, she surrounded by foot soldiers
between fire and deceit

The Sign of the Arch
I count the bracelets in your arms, and distill silence so it can sprout
Prepare feasts for the travelers
And lift from the saddles of the wind:
whatever, and whenever
The flasks heave within the soul in awe
And the evening spreads
Perchance I might choose you at the end of a lifetime, a youthful archer

brooding like a female
Who beats on the shells with her gold
So the houses flow with their compartments
As sorrow turns song deaf
Perchance I will choose you toward my end,
and perchance we will
exchange with this dust its guilt
horse by horse.

I AM FATIMA

Translated by Amira Kashgary

*To Fatima and Mansour, who have been forcibly divorced against their will
on the ground of un-equivalent lineage. To their two children who
will endure the pain and agony of this divorce.*

I am Fatima
I call not for waging wars
I pray not for new delusions
Suffice it
To hold onto my small share of humanity
To fiddle with my right to life behind bars.
I claim not that my vision is always right
But I stand by my right to my destiny.
Have I not the right to breathe like all humans?
Is my existence not worthy of its share of oxygen
Imaginary as it may be?
Am I made of a nature different from other human beings?
I don't go far in my dreams
But I hold onto every ounce of my being to be who I am.

I am Fatima
A woman from the land of arid desert and oil
A woman from the land of traditions and holiness
A woman who places her hands, soaked in darkness, on a dream:
To merely live
With her daughter, Nuha; With her son, Sulaiman; and With her
husband, Mansour

I don't ask for more
I don't settle for less

I am Fatima, small but strong on her own
Large with sympathy on my long journey, in the darkness of the jail
I'm living in!!

And with the light of the innate right I carry within all my senses!

Only to live with my small family
Kept in my heart
After my large family, stretching from sea to sea, has lost me.

When I put my small son in my lap
Along that endless prison wall
When I lull him to sleep so that I have some solitude
When I sleep lonely, scattered, and isolated
I feel more love for the life I have chosen,
For the husband I have accepted and
For the children I've begotten.

I am Fatima
Never begging for a bite or for dignity
Never summoning my tears to join that river of larger tears
Never waiting for pity from a soul.

I am Fatima
Only waiting for fellowmen to open a door to my simple rights
To live together with my son, daughter and husband in our little house,
To open our eyes in the morning to a clear sun
As tender on us as young flower buds in this universe.

To fix my daughter's uniform before she sets off to her nursery school
close to my heart

To relieve her father from carrying her on his shoulders throughout
the times I was lost in the dungeons and charities

For Sulaiman and Nuha to laugh listening to their father's songs

Or to have them laugh at a family love quarrel between their parents

I am Fatima
I seek not to wage war on anyone

I hope not for a fight between the trees and their branches
Or between the flowers and their roots

I merely march on toward my humanity
Which has been written in the lines of a true love story
Toward a marriage blessed by my father
Together with my future husband!!

I am Fatima
A tree in this open space
I monopolize neither "righteousness" nor truth,
I explain not why the stars sleep near dawn
I open my eyes on nothing but what makes the world happier, more
transparent, and more just,
I am the innocent daughter of this country
And its true seed
I don't take of its air more than I need
I don't see of the sky further than what's enough for me
And for my simple freedom
I don't open my eyes on more dewy blueness than I need
To embrace my son, my daughter, and my husband.

I am Fatima
With my own hand I've chosen my poison and my medicine
With my own fingers I've opened my cell
Inside me I carried my son
Till he came into the dark prison night,
Sharing with his mother the harsh realities and details of this place

. . .

When Sulaiman smiles
Hope rekindles in my withered branches,
When he cries, I feel the walls of my vanishing jail cell,
The day his sister Nuha is allowed to visit me, we will celebrate our
wedding under the shades of the black walls,
We will open our windows to "a hope incurable"
That we will unite together
A father, a mother and their two little children
In joyous freedom of hope,
In sorrows of the present and flowers of future smiles.

I am Fatima
Not calling for war
Not calling for peace
Not calling for condemnation nor for dispute,
That is not for me,

But I raise my wounded voice
For the wind to hear
For voices of all times to recount,
To remain in power in the open places I'm deprived of

I am Fatima
I stand by my right to life
My right to love, and my right to live with my children and my husband
As all birds live peacefully in their nests!

A KISS

Translated by Issa J. Boullata

If I had a pen
it would write a book
about the rapture of roses
as they rise from their beds
and walk with eagerness
to kiss the belle
laughing into the lips of a cell phone
whispering in the garden's lanes.

A MOON

Translated by Issa J. Boullata

If I had a moon
I would give its attributes as a present
to the sky
and I would strew a slim summer
of its wheat and shepherds
over the girls going to the fields,
I would draw its blue
on the lamps of the houses
and remain alone
dozing
in the darkness of dreams

ASHJAN AL HENDI was born in Jeddah, Saudi Arabia. She earned her doctoral degree from the Department of Language and Arabic Literature at the School of Oriental and African Studies of the University of London. Her first poetry collection was *Dream Smell of Rain* (1996). Others include *Rain Has a Taste of Lemon* (2007) and, most recently, *Riq al-Ghaimat* (2010). She has also published a book of criticism, *Engagement with Heritage in the Contemporary Poetry of Women in the Arabian Peninsula* (1996). She is currently an assistant professor of Modern Arabic Literature in the Department of Arabic Language and Literature, King Abdulaziz University.

BUTTERFLIES

Translated by Issa J. Boullata

When the man-lamp
shines
the colorful butterflies gather around him
And when he is extinguished
they collect their colors
and go searching
for another lamp

A COUPLE

Translated by Ashjan Al Hendi and Patty Paine

The poem comes stealthily—
A beauty seeking the comfort of my closeness.
So I draw close,
And she reveals her face.
She draws close,
And I reveal the surface of my door
In a small spot of light.
Under my window,
On the violet's dew,
We spread secrets
And whispers.
We sit among the violets
And throw our intentions on the petals of roses
We throw in our grief
And mix it with time, read as pomegranates.
We mix it well,
And drink what we have made.
Us too;
The water fell on us too,
So we became one,
Intertwined like branches dotted with white flowers.
Deprived of dreams, we sat
Side by side, our words imbued
With the glory of basil.
We emerged from its yawn,
She emerged into the tender embrace
Of companions.
She promised to return.
I emerged and searched for a surrogate.
She did not return.

Her tenderness was lost to me.
I replaced her company with sleep.
I fell against the dew drops,
The door remained ajar,
And time took the same path we took.

GRAY HAIR

Translated by Abdulla Al-Harrasi, with Adrian Roscoe

Jasmine fixed its heart in her braid
a flowering rivulet
touched her hair
the flavor of perfume
slept on her breath
rose quarreled over the bouquet of her laugh
She glanced at her face in the mirror
dissolving the show of its sugar
surveying the pallor of her blueness
she arranged the wave of her gown
she fixed the color of her posture
her branches are preparing now
for dancing among her attractions
she knows that the branches of roses
are broken by the fire of their jealousy
and that violet has courted her
to share with it her charm
and the pink flower has deceived her
to share with it her secret
she knows that time's pursuing her
drunk with the goblets of her end
and she knows
her life's story would be shrouded
when her mirror's tears
mourn the gray hair in her braid.

I Swear by the God of *Al-Kawthar*
Translated by Abdulla Al-Harrasi, with Adrian Roscoe

I swear by the God of *Al-Kawthar**
I would love you like London's rain:
Turbulent and clamorous
Sudden and pouring
Even in summer.
I would love you
With Parisian chic:
Blending chocolate brown
With the redness of wine
Scenting coffee with jasmine.
And I would love you like the Dutch:
Join branches of roses
To the bosom of violets.
Like Mexico too:
I would dip your body in my spices
Grill you in my body's fiery longing.
I would love you in the tropical manner:
Burn in you to melt my wounds
And cool to appease your fire
In the forests of my soul.
I would love you
In the manner of Native Americans:
Decorate my head with your feathers
Dance round your fire with clamor.
I would love you in the way of Africa:
Scribble your looks like tribal marks
On the brownness of my seeking.
I would love you as pharaohs loved lotus
And papyrus,
And hunt your heart with one shot

A shot that is my own.
I embalm your feelings
As they climax their flow toward me;
Your heart will never escape alive
So choose the kohl of your mummy.
I would love you like a Bedouin:
Master travel between
The tents of your heart.
I would love you in the feudal manner:
Own you and divide you amongst myself.
And in the Cowboy way:
Shoot you
If you tried to flee from the grip of my breath.
I want to love you with silent clamor
And with clamorous silence.
I would love you like sufi love for love soul light
And sublime purity of the cosmos
Only glorifying God's kingdom.
I swear by the God of *Al-Kawthar*
That I'd love you with the floods of many mysterious rivers
And I'd love you in a way
Never mastered
By sheikh of sufi *tariqah*.**

*Al-Kawthar: name of a river in Paradise.
**Tarkiqah: religious brotherhood, dervish order.

IN SEARCH OF THE OTHER

Translated by Ashjan Al Hendi

Isabella*
She searches for someone else every day;
     and finds me
   And I search for someone else;
     but find her
It is said: that East and West shall never meet
     but Isabella and I
     Meet every day
on our trip in search of others.

*Isabella is a German girl who was a member of the Organizing Committee
in charge of the Arab delegation guests participating in the
International Frankfurt Book Fair in 2004.

IT HAS EARS

Translated by Abdulla Al-Harrasi, with Adrian Roscoe

The lungs* of our house
are bigger than our neighbors'.
The coughing of our house
is louder than our neighbors'.
Our neighbors' house
has ears
and the coughing of our house
never stops.

*The Arabic word *sadr* translates as both "lungs" and "chest".

MOON WARS

Translated by Laith al-Husain, with Alan Brownjohn

~

His moon is waning
and mine is full
What the sky chooses for its moons
will be final
We'd be eclipsed
if they brought us down to earth
We'd wane
We'd uncover
the vices of the world
get familiar
with earth's sins
Then we'd swear
that love up there
was purer
And when my footsteps tired
I'd let him carry half the earth's
burden of sands
we'd go together
prisoners of our mistakes
suspicious
falling into each other
dazzling
But utterly exhausted.

I'd ask him
About the nectar
of the question
how the secret kindles the mind
how it revolves on embers
how it is savored

in the cups of the greedy
I'd ask him
whose fault it is
that we should be dragged
into the agony of fire
ourselves ablaze
and whose fault it is
in the slumber of the seas
who is the torturer
that laid the fire
who released the night among the tents.
Truly, love's face is clear now
Pour out your passion in the spirit
Or bid farewell to patience
Let's return to the road of crescents
if you like
And if you don't
draw the wound out of its sheath
And rest on its edge
Reason out with the dubious
The secretive,
The candid,
suppress the breasts of the suspicious
Release the siege from the clouds
And should you accuse me now of erring
I would not wonder
Would not weep
Would not go away
to waters other than that of the galaxies
I won't drink
from your tears
Why does my heart tell me
while the caravan is
behind the remnants of darkness
that questioning is my doom?

that you and I were neither fair
nor treated fairly
were not satisfied
with what the Bedouin moon has given us
and what we drank of its barrenness
and that we did not celebrate
what we had poured into its heart
and exposed of its faults
I ask myself
Why did the full moon tell me
that you are still loyal to its love
and that my accomplishment
cannot screen
the moon's full brilliance in your eyes
the magic of its power
because you are of the moon
you go back to it
and because I am the fruit
of oppression, barrenness and clouds
of war and peace,
of dream and wakefulness
because I am crooked
the apple of temptation
the basil leaves of sin
when I am touched by oppression
I'll beget
only seeds of temptation
that invade your good seasons
defiling your hands
sharing with you the fertile flame
Because God has created me from my own fascination
from the yearning of your soul for love
and fashioned me
from the hunger of your spine for
sin
Thus God has fashioned me

Because I am from you
I'll come to you with all the grace
God has fashioned me with
With all that I've never revealed
never spoken
never obtained
I'll come to you from my grief
From my nothingness
From my pain
From my regret
My arms
My feet
Choosing from my own impetuousness
what I choose
and tempt you until evening
whimpers
and seek your temptation until you are
intoxicated
and the sins of men
dance and prance around you
and I'll slay them
planet
after planet.

ABIR ZAKI has lived, worked, and studied in Paris, Beirut, Kabul, Istanbul, Mecca, Jeddah, and the US. She has a Master's degree in Education in Learning Difficulties from New York, US and a Bachelor's degree in English Language and Literature from Jeddah, Saudi Arabia. She published her first volume of poetry, *Poetic Aroma*, in 2004 and her second, *Wings of Freedom*, in 2008.

AND YOU CALL ME A FEMINIST ...!
Translated by Abir Zaki and Patty Paine

Not like the French
who play liberal and tolerant
or like Marxists
who sexed me radical and essential
nor am I like Barbie
or the woman you want me to be . . .

Like women everywhere,
I expose
but change differently
I am filled with hidden treasures
for eyes to see
the wrong and the rights
sins and the virtue
obedience and rebellion
veiled and the uncovered . . .

In my truth lies a timeless reality
changing my attitudes and ideas
for whatever I am is never enough

as long as the mortal sin of righteous
and extremes exists!

I'm unequally equaled
for in the depth of my soul
lies the true me
with all my
shamelessness and boldness
insolence and impudence
wantonness and wickedness,
and with all my
devious immorality . . .

I wonder how you perceive
me when you see my face
or hear the words I speak
or read the words I inscribe
A woman of strength or pain?
A woman of love or who is lost?
Or a woman who scares
and confuses you with her words?

Or perhaps you do not see me at all
the woman of affection
who has felt pain
who gets lost within her thoughts?
the one who is proud to be a woman
of many things
for it shows I am alive
I see me for who I am
but I need air
for I am barely breathing . . .

Because I am who I am . . .
but hidden

BUT SHE IS NEVER A LOSER . . .
Translated by Abir Zaki and Patty Paine

When her torch burns and sings,
She is a Goddess . . .
When she is vicious and vindictive,
She is a Harridan . . .
When she is holy and pure,
She is a Virgin . . .
When she gets angry at them,
And rediscovers herself,
She is a Feminist . . .
When she takes him for better and worse,
She is a Wife . . .
When she calms his hurricanes,
And soothes his passion,
She is a Lover . . .
When she sacrifices herself,
She is a Mother . . .
When she finds happiness in solitude,
She is a Spinster . . .
When she prays, begs, and pleads,
She is a Nun . . .
When she walks in the streets,
And earns at night,
She is a Lady of Pleasure . . .
When she wears a red dress,
With a purple hat,
And sits on the street
To take a breath
She is an old lady . . .

But she is never a loser, never a failure . . .
That is what she is,
That is how she is,
Simple and Plain . . .

FOWZIYAH ABU-KHALID, born in Riyadh, holds a BA in Sociology from Lewis & Clark College, Portland, Oregon, an MA in Sociology from King Saud University, Riyadh, Saudi Arabia, and a PhD in Political Sociology from the University of Salford, Manchester, UK. Since 1974, she has published five poetry collections and two books of children's literature. Her work has been included in several Arabic, German, and English anthologies and she has presented her academic work at conferences worldwide. She has participated in numerous international poetry festivals, readings, and conferences and has served on the faculty at King Saud University for thirty years.

MY LATE HOURS WITH ME

Translated by Ghassan Nasr, with Joseph Heithaus

By five in the morning, I'm always down to the final drop
of the night's river in the glasses of the late hours still with me
All I want then is to sleep for one more hour
before the alarm rings
and pulls me by my eyelashes to work
With no appointment and no prior warning
there's a knock at the door
I barely hear it as sleep wrings me out
and I fall back to sleep
but the knocking doesn't stop
The poem climbs to my windows
by the tendrils of my nerves
furtively stretching to it
and it sprays its oil on my fingers
scatters its burning candles
on the bed

And what sort of ink chooses now
to mix with my blood unaware I've just returned from the sea
and have already locked in my veins enough topaz, coral, and waves
I hide from myself in the feathers of a poet
because the sand was made for me alone to splash my ink there
But we leave the room together
to let the woman take off her night clothes
and bring her daytime self to the mirror

CRAVING

Translated by Abdulla Al-Harrasi, with Adrian Roscoe

I loathe cooking
I loathe my bed
I loathe perfume
Especially aftershave
Anointed with my partner's sweat—
He is free from the scent of greed
Every creature's shed its skin
Donned a garlic coat
To chase me with the snake of nausea.
My inside an open wound
Flowing with pus, churning my guts
Shaking my limbs with embryo hauteur.
How could that innocent sperm
With wondrous shifts
From transparent drop
To human torrent
Change me to this temporary carcass?
What slow-burn coal roasts my living meat
With fever of transformation
Till my soul flees my pores
Like burnt plastic?
There's no escape from it or me
However I breathe, it flows full and free.

ACIDITY SMELL

Translated by Abdulla Al-Harrasi, with Adrian Roscoe

Like a flute that leaks *mawawil**
drowned in tears
like a cylinder filled with choking gas
my windpipe flows
with invisible steam
that conquers
my breath
and bites my lungs with solid air.

*Mawwal (pl. *mawawil*): a poem in colloquial language,
often sung to the accompaniment of a reed pipe.

PREGNANCY SMELL

Translated by Abdulla Al-Harrasi, with Adrian Roscoe

No one, no one
whatever the chemical reaction
whatever the elemental mix
could change himself
to a full cylinder
a fruit-heavy tree
fountains, spilling
a riot of scents—
like a woman
her ribs
carved with the bud of genesis.

RIPE DATE SMELL

Translated by Abdulla Al-Harrasi, with Adrian Roscoe

Who can smell ripe dates
except she who passes a river
flowing with Mariam's blood
lying beneath the hoofs of death
stealing life?

LABOR SMELL

Translated by Abdulla Al-Harrasi, with Adrian Roscoe

Whatever the colognes sprayed
whatever antiseptics are poured
however air pollutes or weather clears
if hot simoom winds blow
and breezes wiffle
labor has a monstrous smell
that soul-clings till death—
a tell-tale badge
never to be torn from mothers.

FENUGREEK SMELL

Translated by Abdulla Al-Harrasi, with Adrian Roscoe

This shy plant
with its tender curving stems
and white sleepy heads
owns no power
save the stinking delights
it breathes in the veins
of a woman confined
promising to heal birth wounds.

ANISE SMELL

Translated by Abdulla Al-Harrasi, with Adrian Roscoe

I'm faint from gentle numbness
spreading through my nerves
with vapor cloud threads
rising from the anise cup.
My wounds completely heal
when the smell-spell fills me
when the drink comes close to my mouth.

BABY SMELL

Translated by Abdulla Al-Harrasi, with Adrian Roscoe

Neither the anise nor the fenugreek
nor my husband's sudden kindness
not even amnesia itself
can make me forget the hour of death
so deceptively called the hour of birth.
I smell my baby
the fragrance of paradise
laurel that laurel would envy
and I'm cured by iodine of the sea
spreading from the silk in my breast

241

TUFUL: NOONDAY RAINBOW

Translated by Ruanne Abou-Rahme and Patricia Alanah Byrne

I open the book of poetry
   Or the valves of the heart
What poem can contain
   The gentle waving of your
Little hand at the school door?
What rhythm can retain the movement of your little feet
And the swishing of your uniform
   As you flit
Between the street and my heart?
The noon sun kindles your hair
your chestnut hair kindles the noon sun
with rainbow colors
You throw the heavy schoolbag off your little
shoulders
like a branch getting free of its weight of apples
And I can hear the fluttering of the feathers
on the wings,
You take off your school shoes
And a river of holy ink pours on the slate of my fate
   You come near . . . you jump
you give me a kiss that pours the anxiety of poets
   in my veins,
etches the miracle of the scene
fleeting like a boundless colt.

TWO LITTLE GIRLS

Translated by Jinan M. Coulter and Patricia Alanah Byrne

I hang on the tail of her dress
as a little boy
hangs
to the thread of
a rising kite
　I climb her braid
as a squirrel climbs
the branch of a hazelnut tree
We hop in the open deserts from one world to the next
reroute ourselves with every gust of air
　like birds just freed from a cage
Move from one game to another
And she teaches me
　the names of flowers
　the seasons of rain
　the love of country
And I teach her

　obstinacy and mischief
We share one apple
　and innumerable dreams
We paint with the desert a paradise of questions
sprinkle each other
　with mirage water
　and befriend a fleeting gazelle
and when sunset surprises us
the doors open their jaws like ogres
in the inscrutable twilight

And who can solve
The mystery?
Which is the mother
Which the child?

NUMERICAL CONJECTURE
Translated by Ghassan Nasr, with Joseph Heithaus

Six
Seven
Nine
These are not numerical symbols
They are not dates of defeats or chronicles of victories
and not
a language for measuring the calendar's arithmetic
or for marking an early punishment or a delayed reward
My memory is betrayed
by monotonous math classes
with their yawning lessons
and me leaving through the bolted window
without the teacher sensing anything
except the unruly winds
the source of which she fears
I surrender my withered body
to the surprises of the number six
Days not yet titled
Names the angels
have not yet heard
A universe coming into existence all at once
Mountains not yet arched from the ground or chiseled out
Fresh hearts not yet worthy of betrayal
Soil where blood has not been spilled
Prey not yet caught
A moon whose beauty hasn't been defiled by metaphors
A bride who hasn't been snatched away
A sun so new it has never set
Pride that has not been humbled
And no sooner do I reach seven

than the seventh day arrives
Friday night or Sunday morning appears
announcing a time of rest
forbidding any wandering in regions beyond the week
One sudden current follows another
and pacifies my fears of the shudder of discovery
Slowly, slowly
what is known in my blood coagulates bit by bit
almost transforms into encumbering custom
I stretch my body on grass dulled
by the rolling of lovers
I start a morning with a sunrise
exhausted from the repetitions of a summer
I collide with a night wrinkled by ages of sleep
I ask for water and a glass
comes to me smeared with the rouge of lips
I travel and the horizons are blocked
by checkpoint gates
and at those edges I am hounded
by the curse of my olive skin
The teacher hooks me by the waist
with her fishing rod of numbers
and pulls me up without me being prepared
The exam:
Recite the multiplication tables
A pregnant woman screeches
as her labor pains have come
Valleys spill from the narrows of her pelvis
I shake a palm tree
Its roots are only in my memory
A new existence dawns to destroy my previous experience
The unknown mocks what I had imagined to be
answers new questions
I start back to school again
and begin pronouncing the ABCs

sensing joys I hadn't known
I try writing with the ink of my mother's milk
Six days
Seven skies
Nine months

ABDALLAH AL SAIKHAN of Saudi Arabia has been the editing director of *Al Yamamah* magazine and the vice-president and editor-in-chief of the daily Arabic newspaper *Okaz*. His first poetry collection, *Concerns among a nation's weather*, was published in 1988 by Dar Al Adab, Beirut, with a second edition published by the Hail Literary Club. Subsequent collections include *The Return of Imru' Al Qais* and *Neglected Poems*. He has participated in numerous poetry and cultural events in Saudi Arabia and in several conferences both within and outside the Arab world. His poetry has been translated into English under the auspices of PROTA, the Project for the Translation from Arabic.

STAR OF INK

Translated by Ayesha Saldhana

Ours, a high moon in Al Yamama
But when we stay awake, he comes down the stairs in the sky
to pass the night

Ours, the star of ink . . .
We write it, and the heavens are a notebook

Ours, in the pigeons, the cooing of two . . .
But their tears turned to stone

Ours, in infatuation, an orphan's heart . . .
But when it loves passionately, I flourish

Ours, Imru Al Qays, seeking a lost country . . .
Then he loses

Ours, in Al Rasafa, two flutes . . .
Sorrow keeps us distant . . . until we gather our souls in
a book of scattered satires

Ours, two glasses, in remorse
I spilt the more beautiful once upon a sorrow
And the second of them broke

Ours . . . nothing but this hell that has surrounded us . . .
But, from the dew, it will uncover

Ours, God
And God is great.

THE POET
Translated by Ayesha Saldhana

He rejoices . . . Thirty rivers of silk and a forest of aquamarine
belong to him
A desert belongs to him, when she spirals swiftly behind the wind
and a rebelling boxthorn
Water belongs to him, since a cloud – lightly – passed by . . .
and the prairie rejoiced
Poetry belongs to him, since rhymes were suspended over the
spinning wheel of black wool
He rejoices . . . Thirty broken mirrors and a thousand
unfurled verses belong to him.

SWORD
Translated by Ayesha Saldhana

The days were summer
I was sitting on the roof, and the trees were telling me what
the river had generously granted them
With praise, and rustling

I said, Mother, speak some poetry for me
She drew a sword on the ground
And said it was a palm leaf.

MALIHA

Translated by Ayesha Saldhana

Her face is rain . . . and her hands are dust
This which grows on her shoulders has fruit, like absence
Her face is rain
Her chest is two clouds of clarity, or a dream of two children
Or a nation within, in its possibilities: rain . . . no rain
Maliha awoke when the morning came; she wore her house robe
and turned to song
Rain . . . no rain
She lifted her face to the sky
Rain . . . no rain
And undressed as birds do
The sky granted her its windows
It rained . . . rained
And Maliha was suspended over the trees.

THURAYA AL ARRAYED of Saudi Arabia received her BA in Education
from the Beirut College for Women, her MA in Educational Administration
from the American University of Beirut, and her PhD in Educational
Administration and Planning from the University of North at Chapel Hill,
US. A well-known thinker, poet, writer, and literary figure, Dr. Al Arrayed
is an active researcher in the literary, educational, and total development
fields, and has participated in high-profile specialized national, regional,
Arab, and international forums and conferences, such as Davos, Arab
Thought forums, the World Petroleum Congress, the Arab Media Summit,
and literary festivals in all Arab countries. She writes several regular
columns in Saudi, Arabian Gulf, and Arab newspapers and has three
published volumes of poetry. Her poems have been translated into several
languages and are included in several anthologies.

DESERT DREAMS

I came into your world
Wrapped in my inherited desert shawls
All my ancestors nomadic uncontrollable souls
An immense mysterious heritage
Do you comprehend what that implies
When you ask me to swap a desert's infinite horizon
With a one way trip to a door and walls?

I come with no promises
Freezing nights
Scorching sun
Misleading mirages
scant showers
obstinate blooming flowers
And unpredictable sand storms

It is the wasteland heritage
Ruling our realities, truths, and lies

I come into your world
With spring blooms
Enchanting your bewildered yearning fascinated eyes
Yet nothing but thorny thirst
In their questions of existence and replies
Nothing but thirst
In the folds of their silky sighs

I will be truthful as I hear your thoughts and dreams
Nothing is really what it seems
Because we see it with desire in our eyes.

Don't dream that you will rule my ever moving dunes
Or that you will ever own the keys to my mysterious tunes

My heart is a desert mystic conversing with stars
Do you understand
As you eye the golden sand
How vast its boundaries really are?

Do you understand
What I am and what you are?

All your promises
All the springs of your being
Will not produce an everlasting Eden in my eyes

You are here in passing
Like all the caravans before
Enjoy your fleeting moments of a desert spring
And do not ask for more

Enjoy the fleeting fickle moments like the desert mirage
And then
We will not cry when you or I are gone
You will be gone
No one thrives forever
Under the desert's glaring truthful sun.

THE DOORS; THE GAME OF TIMES

Every day
When the enchanted time's child shares my solitude
She lifts me with fatal calmness
Out of the orbit of the four seasons
Through the worn out doors
Searching for the fifth Season
Where dreams should have poured.

You didn't come in Summer . . .
Nor in the Spring before
(Spring was long, exhausting and confusing
like a teenager's yearning for a neighbor
Whose shadow penetrates curtained windows, thundering rainless
storms, while waiting for the lights in her room to go off,
and hoping for a smile that never materialized.)

An eternal sadness inhabits rusting doors
When they stop in the turn of time
Freezing motionless
Behind them you are not alone to let go of your tears
Nor are you with others
To force your eyelids to hold the tears in.

℞⊃

You didn't come in summer
And you will not come in the fall

(Nothing really comes in the fall except our
Illusions . . .
The green caterpillars breeding incessantly
Devouring the leaves of the Nabaq tree
while we polish our dreams against the
inevitability of losing hope as we wait)

℞⊃

The game of Times
Our legacy: the cruelty of the known unknown
The beginnings, the ends . . .
The possibility of confused seasons . . .
Some of the cocoons never achieve the wings of butterflies.

℞⊃

You did not come in summer
And you will not in fall
When the winds play with the leaves
They surrender in whirlwinds of pale yellow
Collapsing like the tired moths at the end of the night
Like our internal tears glistening behind the doors

℞⊃

An eternal sadness inhabits the rusted doors
It is impossible to close them against the jarring wind.
Joy is not seeable when the fog of sadness dulls the visionary spirit,
foreboding a lurking threat to the hopeful cocoons.

❧

You did not come in the spring
And will definitely not come in the freezing winter.

And if you do the door will latched securely
In the face of winter blizzards
The gates will be buried deep in the snow of time
And I will not hear you
If you knock on the door
Nobody will open.

❧

The tearful child
Remembers the characters of familiar tales
She checks the doors and the worn out pages
There is no fifth season except in our yearnings
And children's tales

❧

The myths of the fifth season

lock time in an enchanted spring time
Where the doors never rust.
Cinderella crosses into it in the golden pumpkin coach
And leaves at the twelfth strike of midnight
Sleeping Beauty awakens to the kiss of passing stranger
Snow White the dwarf's beloved soul sister survives a coma
induced by an apple poisoned in hate.
And Beauty is finally convinced that her kiss will turn
a beast into a prince

❦

The little girl lost behind the doors is tired
checking me with the eyes of a woman
Whose spring grayed prematurely with snow
She knows that the doors have rusted
And that there is no fifth season in the game of times

❦

You did not come in Spring!

. . .

and the doors have rusted
Why?
Why didn't you come in Spring?

MOMENTS OF SILENCE

Just for these sweeping moments
Glorious unforeseen
Unknown companion
Stay unknown
Let me not know you; Who you are
Or who you might have been
The hands that threw you here across my way
Will in a while pull you away again

Just for these moments
As our shadows melt
As our footsteps echo softly in the sand
Say nothing
We – who're here but for a day–
Cannot demand
We come commanded
And depart too by command

Say nothing!
Ask not who I am
Talk not of our place
Or our time
Talk not of yesterday,
– bitter or sweet–
Talk not of worlds to be
Or ways to meet.

Just now, this meeting point
Of nowhere in no time
These precious moments
Are for us to share

Strangers before we met
And strangers as we stand
Lost in a twilight of awareness
Hand in hand
Just as we are
Companion, share my world with me
Before our strings are pulled too far.
No time for talking
No time to explain
No time to think of happiness or pain

Companion as I am now
As you are
Silently share a smile, a tear
And when it's time to go
Silently . . . disappear.

The Stillborn

I want to burst, to shout
Speak up with all my force
With all my might
Open my swollen heart
Cry out
Until the word is heard
Until the word pierces the sky

I suffocate
I'm heavy with the word
I'm pregnant with the word
Enclosed within my soul
Unknown . . . unheard
I suffocate
I'd turn to any passerby
To any stranger
Any sullen face
And call:
Here brother, look at me;
look deep into my eyes
Into my heart
Brother, companion
We are free!
Why do we separate?
Why think in terms of you and me?
Think of the Whole
Of every human soul
Break down the wall
And reach your hand to me.

Come to my bosom, Mate
Let not these masks keep us apart.
I die to see
A loving smiling face
For I am you and you are I
Open your heart and stronger we shall grow
Then we shall find the way
Easy to go
Together we shall go

I want to cry
To shout
To bring the struggling message out
Yet I am coldly stopped by staring eyes.
That look of vagueness
Wild surprise

I see a world of emptiness
A world of loneliness
Of broken ties
Not to be mended
Far beyond repair
A world where no one dares
To call another, friend

I see within the frozen staring eyes
A universe of ugliness
Of fear of despair
I see the shadows cast
By centuries of hate

And then the word
The struggling word
Silently dies
Within my boiling breast.

GHAZI AL GHOSAIBI was born in al-lhsa' in 1940 in eastern Saudi Arabia. He had his early education in Bahrain, then obtained a BA in Law from the University of Cairo in 1961. In 1964, he obtained an MA in International Relations from the University of Southern California, US, and in 1970 a PhD in Political Science from the University of London, UK. He held important positions in his country's government, becoming the Minister of Industry and Electricity (1976–1983), Minister of Health (1983–1985), and ambassador to Bahrain and to the UK. At the time of his death in 2010, he was the Saudi Arabian labor minister. His many books in print include *Verses of Love* (1975), *You Are My Riyadb* (1976), *Fever* (1980), and *Chosen Poems* (1980).

DUSTING THE COLOR FROM ROSES
Translated by A. A. Ruffai and Heather Lawton

Autumn's lust touches
trees, impregnating
horizons with gales,
storms and darkness.

Autumn moves further—
tastes humans,
causing hearts to shiver
with the fear of death
And the longing to be born.

Meanwhile, I stood in the black forest
nursing ennui, and watching as horizons
struggled to give birth to children.

My lady,
My lady,
O summer, which flamed upon me
out of season. In your eyes I saw
(what a splendid paradox) a full moon
sailing across a sea gleaming like the moon.

I heard all the songs of the pearl—
divers and the shepherds; as summer
drags you, once more, toward the harvest,
(And I, insomniac, am dragged along behind.)

My lady,
My lady,
My song is painful.
My sobs disturb the strings
of the lutes, making the music ignite.
As in the Ode of as-Sayyab, when he cried alone
in the rain;
or the cries of al-Mutanabbi, as he threw
his life into the night,
over the villain's horses,
or the tears of Naji
as he lamented the stones
painting ruins with ashes.

My lady,
My lady,
My song is the cry
of every poet transcending
centuries with his poetry,
only to die alone,
a stranger in the desert.

My lady,
My lady,
Who placed an obituary
outlined in black
on the first page of a newspaper
to inform us that autumn
had committed suicide?

Just think about it, lady,
what if autumn took over everything
leaving nothing but memories in the forest
of green plants on their knees?

Just contemplate autumn draining
summer from windows;
dusting the color from roses.
It is autumn, the lord of all seasons,
bearing secrets of survival and loss;
of death and of resurrection.

IN THE OLD STREET

Translated by A. A. Ruffai and Heather Lawton

We return
    To the street which long ago
Our home overlooked.

We ask it
    About the years of our love.
And longing glistens on its lips.

We ask it
    About those years when we were young.
And its eyes burn with tears.

A quarter of a century or more has passed.
    And that young man has changed
And changed and changed . . .

Then his mind was pure and brilliant.
    And he was a better poet,
He plunged his dagger into the heart of conflicts.
    Until the dagger broke.
And he sailed his ship fearlessly
    Into the eye of the storm until he drifted
    and was wrecked.

He roamed the deserts with his passionate heart,
    Until that too ossified and
He returned, dragging the ruins of his years behind him,

To produce these recycled poems you read.
　　See, here is the restaurant of yesterday,
Serving the same obscene food.

Here is the bookseller, selling the same old books,
　　Around the corner lies the same dust,
　　the same smells
And children, just as crazy and wild as before, playing.

Our house is just the same as it always was—
　　Even down to the daily newspapers
And milk delivered before dawn breaks.

Tell me this – why do men grow old,
　　Old and gray, while the streets remain
The same as they always were, are now, and will be?

Now at the door I am tempted to ring the bell.

OH, DESERT

Translated by Anne Fairbairn and Ghazi Al-Gosaibi

I've searched the world without finding
land more barren,
love more pure,
or rage more fierce than yours.
I came back to you, oh desert,
sea-spray on my face;
in my mind, a mirage of tears,
a shadow moving in the sea before
dawn and a golden flash of braided hair.
On my lips, two lines of poetry a song without echo.

I came back to you, disenchanted.
I've found there's
no trust between human beings.
I came back to you deprived;
the world's like a rib cage
without a heart.
Love is a word devoid of love.
I came back to you defeated;
I've been fighting life's battles
with a sword forged from feeling.

I came back to you . . . and laid my anchor
on the sand.
As I washed my face with dew
it seemed you were calling me.
Then you whispered:
"Have you come back to me, my child?"
Yes . . . mother . . . I came back to you.
A child, forever grieving,

flew to God's countries;
unable to find his nest,
he came back to search for his life in you.

I came back to you, oh desert.
I've thrown away my quiver and ceased wandering,
I dally in your night-web
of mystery,
breathing on the soft winds of the *Najd*
the fragrance of *Araar*.
In you I live for poetry and moons.

WHICH ONE OF US RETURNED SAFELY?
Translated by A. A. Ruffai and Heather Lawton

In memory of my friend, the late Qasim Ibn Muhammad Algosaibi

In the summit
of the years past
I take refuge
from the unexpected
events hidden by time.

O brother
at a point in life
when time
was delicious,
striding leisurely,
like an idle beauty.

O brother
of poetry
when it rhymes
were celebration
after celebration
of living.

O brother
of the full moon,
elated stars,
and the evening
strung with pearls;
was that a parting?

But have we not
had our fill of parting?
In a life
too stingy
to offer us reunion.

Was that a farewell?
For every night
there is a morning;
save for the murderous
night of dying.

I close my eyes,
but I do not see you in pain
coiled on the grip
of clattered weapons.
I do not see
the yellowness of death
on your cheeks
beneath the shadow of sorrow
and the incision of arrow-heads.

I see my old friend
youthful, carefree.
(Does vigor ever care?)
I close my eyes,
mount the back of dreams
(some dreams are not illusions).

My thoughts cross the Nile
when friends
of early youth
were present
and you were near me.

Death grasps almost everything,
but fails in taking
away my dearest memories.
O Qasim,
the one tortured
by life . . .
A life which loves
to ravish men,
sipping from our blood
whatever we drank
from its draught of elegance
in the tavern
of horrors.

Which one of us
returned safely?
The one pierced
with poverty;
or the one pierced
with riches?
Life may unleash
a sword of glory;
But victims
make the rallies
of heroes.

Which one
of us came back safely?
We are locked
in a struggle
between the sexton
and the buried.

And the bitter harvest
smolders, burning
ember on the eyes.

O Qasim,
the one tortured
by people and
by gossip.
Which one of us returned safely
Amid the informers,
the hypocrites,
the deceitful liars?
Which one of us returned safely?
Proximity equals
remoteness;
and company,
solitude.
Our tranquility
is the mercy of God.
Take comfort in it
after the horror of the fight.

POETS FROM THE UNITED ARAB EMIRATES

The United Arab Emirates is a confederation of Arab states comprised of Abu Dhabi, Dubai, Ajman, Fujairah, Ras al Khaimah, Sharjah, and Umm al Qaiwain. Bordering Oman and Saudi Arabia, it has a population of about five million. Twenty percent of those are Emiri nationals, with the rest being primarily expatriates and workers. Each of the states is a monarchy, ruled by various families, with the head of state of the UAE, the president, being the emir of Abu Dhabi, and the head of government, the prime minister, being the emir of Dubai. Although its main sources of revenue are oil and international banking, its recent focus has been on ways to improve education and employment opportunities for its citizens. Its widely varied population makes it among the most diverse and multicultural societies in the Gulf.

NUJOOM ALGHANEM, both a poet and prize-winning filmmaker, was born in Dubai, UAE. Following a career as a journalist for the Abu Dhabi newspaper *Almaraa Alyaum*, she earned a degree in television production from Ohio University, US and a Master's degree in Film Production from Griffith University School of Film in Australia. Alghanem has made five documentary films, including *Hamam*, centered around a famous Emiri female shaman who is recognized across the Gulf region for her contribution toward saving hundreds of souls from different kinds of illness (2010); *Between Two Banks* (1999), based on the story of Khamees Marzouq, the last remaining rowing boatman on Dubai Creek; and *Al Mureed*, about the revered Emirati Sufi Sheikh Abdul Raheem Al Mureed and winner of the Best Documentary in the Gulf from the Emirates Film Competition in Abu Dhabi in 2008. Her seven poetry collections include *Masaa Al-Janah* [Evening of Heaven] (1989); *Al-Jarair* [The Sins] (1991); *Rawahel* [Journeyings] (1996); *Manazel Al-Jilnaar* [Homes of Pomegranate Blossoms] (2000); *La Wasf Lima Ana Feeh* [No Describing What I Am In] (2005); *Malaikat Al-Ashwaaq Al-Baeeda* [Angels of Distant Longing] (2008); and *Layloun Thakilon Alla Allayle* [Heavy Night on the Night] (2010).

BLAZING FIRES

Translated by Khaled Mattawa

Her breathing is a race among her sorrows,
but her voice remains calm before the sea.
There is no window
for her to face
her desire for flight,
not even a hole
through which she can escape
the hell of her solitude.
Night comes along and spreads its kohl

and the groans of its creatures,
causing her to lose all her poise.
Air does not blow before her threshold
and she sees no outlet
for this love hidden under her shirt.
Nowhere to keep it
except inside her notebooks.

IMMIGRANT

Translated by Khaled Mattawa

Since our last morning together
this bird has taken to my balcony
defining the emptiness with his song.
At midmorning
his arousal for his female peaks
and he releases his love toward the trees
and the nests tucked
within cracks in the nearby walls.
He searches for her everywhere
while she
waits for him on her branch
not making a single move
as if she is certain
that he reads her silence
in the way she wishes him to.

THE DARKNESS IS THICK
Translated by Khaled Mattawa

The darkness is thick despite the beaming lights,
the candles are soulless,
and we are besieged by the horizon's dimness.
Which of us will start the conversation?
Which of us
will forgive the other?

MONKS
Translated by Khaled Mattawa

Bells shake their tragedies over the cityscape
as if the hereafter wishes
to rattle the sleepers' confusion.
The monks do not wish to cease their sadness
and they do not want us to sleep.

I Remember Him
Translated by Khaled Mattawa

The winds startle me with their chill
and tears shiver in the corners of my eyes.
I remember him in distant cities
hiding his face in my coat
or warming my ears
or fingers
until our breaths catch fire.
I remember him guarding the shadows of my dreams
when morning rises
or when I rise to his kisses
stamping longings on me
that he could say in words.

By the Seashore
Translated by Khaled Mattawa

She smuggles her longings to the sea
because she knows it will embrace them
like a ship of ether piercing the horizon.

She smuggles her tears to the wind
because the wind is her sister.

DISTANCE

Translated by Khaled Mattawa

He got back in a rush
ready for another departure.
He returned
not to see her,
but to leave her
the key to the house,
a bottle of perfume,
and a few words scribbled
on a shred of paper.
Words meant to keep the peace between them
and that offer love
wings with which
to fly away.

SEAFLOWER

Translated by Khaled Mattawa

The orange moon
dangles like an amulet among the trees
and the clouds barge into the horizon
in rumbling waves.
My eyelids burn
and my vision staggers
as if lost in ash.
Is that the moon
or is it my eyes that can
no longer distinguish
the shapes of things?

THE SNOW OF MOUNTS

Translated by Issa J. Boullata; edited by Elizabeth Thomas

I sit in the very same place
my heart ablaze with yearning
my eyes captivated by the long hallway.
In the very same place
I memorize the faces of passers-by
then let them slip away
like sand through my fingers.

Suddenly his face is thrust among them
and my thoughts stutter.
Do I have to keep him in the cell
or must I open the door for him
to leave?

When I say: I will be careful
my body temperature rises
and the air in the room chills.
As for him, he disappears
between fever
and apprehension.
I think I will be unable
to forget him
yet I go into the alleys like a light feather
with my heart radiant as the snow
of the mounts.

LOYALTY
Translated by Khaled Mattawa

The waves know me when I approach them.
They rush to the shore to sweep
others' footsteps for my sake,
so that I can find a clean place
for my books and papers
a spot that I'll share with no one else.

SHIHAB GHANEM of Dubai is an engineer, a manager, an economist, a poet, and a translator of poetry from Arabic to English and vice versa. He obtained a double degree in Mechanical Engineering and Electrical Engineering from Aberdeen University, UK in 1964, certificates in Industrial Administration and Management of Men (with distinction) from the UK (London and Birmingham universities), a postgraduate diploma and a Master of Engineering degree in Water Resources Development from Roorkee University, India in 1975, and a PhD in Economics in the fields of industrialization and human resources development from Cardiff University, UK in 1989. He has published thirty books, including eight books of poetry in Arabic and one in English, and several volumes of translated poetry, from Arabic to English and from Malayalam and other languages to Arabic via English.

BAKHBOOKH
Translated by Shihab Ghanem

扂

To my granddaughter Hanouf

I centered the coin on my left palm
And blew on it
Then covered it with my other palm
And said to her: "Say *bakhbookh*!"*
She said: "Bah booh"
I opened my hands
Where is the coin? . . . Where? . . .
It vanished in a wink . . .
She laughed . . . astonishment gleamed in her eyes
She was – may God protect her – less than two years old.
"*Bakhbookh*"
And our blown coin vanished

She went and got her big doll,
with the velvet dress.
She put it in my hands and said: "Bah booh"
I said with a hoarse voice:
"This doll is too beautiful to be disappeared,
O soul of my soul!"

Bakhbookh is a word used in some Arab countries in a make-believe
game of making things vanish, like abracadabra.

BEHIND THE IRON CURTAIN
Translated by Shihab Ghanem

I want to cry
But fear stops me, not pride,
On my chest rests a mountain of unhappiness.

I want to ask a question
But it's impossible
For the shadows eavesdrop on every word.

I want to breathe, to be free
Or at least find some sufferable air,
For the chains are eating into the meat of my soul
And I am dying of suffocation.

I want to have a moment of peace
And dream of light born amongst the ruins.
A glimpse of light
Becoming a flood bursting the walls of darkness around me.
But all I hear is laughter resounding
In the pitch blackness,
Mocking me.

I want to have a moment of happiness.
I want . . . and life scoffs at me
And pushes its spear between my ribs

⚮

I want to run away
O! Harder to attain than the feather in the
wing of a flying eagle

Or the glimmer of a mirage
For they have locked a thousand and one doors.

⚮

I want to escape
But how?
When in every corner lies a murdered corpse.

⚮

I want . . . but . . . but . . . but
I shall seek deliverance
Even if blasted by a shower of bullets . . .

ENTRAPPED

Translated by Shihab Ghanem

Because I have realized that poetry achieves nothing
And that I have slaughtered my heart with poetry
And every time a new poem is born, I die a little
I have sworn to write no more

Because I have realized that poetry is devastating, like your love
For both lift me at times to the zenith
And at others toss me into beds of thorns
I have sworn to set myself free,
To tear up my dreams,
To crush my pens,
To banish love
And to lay a bed in my eyelids for sleep . . .
I have decided all this

Yet, I am still entrapped.
I continue to weave the words
And my heart still hovers around your bewitching beauty
And yet I continue to dream
Of plucking roses without thorns
Oh for my poems and for your love!

ILLUMINATIONS IN A VALLEY WITHOUT VEGETATION
Translated by Shihab Ghanem

We have come to You
Repeating: "Here we are, at Your service . . . here we are . . . here we are"
With longing carrying us on wings:
A longing to You
And a longing for Your forgiveness.
We have come to You from all corners of the earth
We have come with an eye on the joys of life
But with both eyes on the bounties of the second life
O Lord! Bestow forgiveness upon us . . .

We have come to You from near and far,
Answering Your call,
Chanting the praise of Your glory
Until our chanting fills the sky.
Walking on land kissed by the feet of prophets.
We have come to You disheveled in our simple attire,
With no adornments and no sewn dresses.
We have come devoid of pride.
We have come with our longing and hopes,
With our overflowing prayers.
We have come with all these crowds, all these millions,
With streams of tears,
Calling You between reverence and praise.
And You are the all-seeing and all-hearing.
We have come with eager steps from all directions
To Mount Arafat
Floating on wings of words of praise for you.
We have come with our love and longing

To cast off the burden of our years into your valley
So Lord accept our repentance and do forgive.

∽

When I stepped into your glorious Grand Mosque
And saw the splendor of your Holy Kaba
I felt a surge of longing in my chest swelling
And felt delight . . . delight . . .
I was drowned in happiness.
I tried to reach the Black Stone
But human waves of Your loving disciples swept me,
And forced me to give up.
So I flew to it with my soul and kissed it like the morning light
And my heart flew to the Moltazem
And when my heart clung to the cover of your Holy Kaba
I felt I was granted a dream . . .
That Your eyes were guarding over me.
When I drank Zamzam water to my heart's fulfillment
I felt I was completely cleansed
And that my heart, which had been parched by sins
Was flowering within my ribs like a rose crowned by morning dew
Diffusing the fragrance of roses.
I was swept by the great moment
The tears running down my cheeks.

Surging angrily, harshly,
As though to welcome violence.
But so long as your image sleeps in my eyelids,
So long as my heart throbs with yearning,
So long as your heart flutters with love,
Then will our love never drown
But forever ride the surf.
And if the waves could come between us . . .
They would dry up!

In our hearts will always be
The song of Love
Despite everything

RADIANCE
Translated by Shihab Ghanem

And when you return to me . . . despite distances . . .
I feel that radiance lighting my face again,
And I hear the sound of sticks in the wheels of my life cracking—
under the radiance,
Under the stars that twinkle in my eyes—
Like thin twigs
I kiss your eyelids . . . while seas and mountains hold us apart
And from the sea I seek inspiration
I read in its every shape a philosophy.
I learn to probe the secrets of serenity
And to realize the turbulence of wrath
And on the dancing waves I witness a new charm
of the full moon
As it breaks into glittering fragments.
Thence I understand restlessness . . .

And how sleeplessness enhances the beauty of
your drooping lids.
I kiss your eyelids . . .
But the seas and mountains remain
And every mountain touched by my gaze inspires
me with the meaning of loftiness,
And the philosophy of patience and endurance.
And when the arms encircle you
After yearning . . .
When time yields, but place does not . . .
I hug my longing to my chest
And wonder how within my arms the two incompatibles unite
The heights of violence . . . and extreme tenderness—
And thence I do not feel the length of distance . . .

. . . The seas . . .
. . . The waves . . .
. . . The night . . .
. . . Or the mountain heights . . .
I only feel the radiance invading my soul
And the exuberance of beauty.

HIS HIGHNESS SHEIKH MOHAMMED BIN RASHID AL MAKTOUM was born in Dubai, UAE in 1947. His education began with private tutoring in Arabic and Islamic studies, and he completed his education in both Dubai and the UK. He became the Emir of Dubai in 2006 following the death of Sheikh Maktoum bin Rashid Al Maktoum. Shortly thereafter he became the Prime Minister and Vice President of the UAE. He writes primarily in the traditional *nabati* style, his poems treating the variety of *nabati* subjects – pride and chivalry, for example – in an apparently spontaneous fashion. He has published several collections of poetry, most recently *Poems from the Desert* (Motivate, 2009).

I PICTURED THE DREAMS – RASHID AND HAMDAN

*This poem was written on the occasion of the graduation of Sheikh Mohammed's
two eldest sons, Sheikh Rashid and Sheikh Hamdan, from the
Royal Military Academy in Sandhurst, England.*

Rashid and Hamdan, the dreams of a bright tomorrow
And I pictured the dreams – Rashid and Hamdan

One named after the one whose name is bounty
The other named after Hamdan bin Zayed Al Nahyan*

People of high rank, their name renowned
Heroes in kindness, and in adversity also heroes

Saw them, in my mind, whilst still in cradle
As leaders of justice and loyalty

And raised them as a lion his cubs
Lanners, never prey for hunters

Hour by hour, guided them to the goal
A father advising his children, shaping men

Rashid, I prepared for dark nights
And pride, Hamdan, purpose and vision

I congratulated, by them, Zayed, to whom they pledge allegiance
And congratulated Maktoum, the people of Dubai, and brothers

*Sheikh Mohammed's maternal grandfather, who was the ruler of Abu Dhabi from 1912 to 1922.

POEM OF CONDOLENCE

*To His Royal Highness Prince Salman bin Abdul Aziz on the
death of Prince Ahmed bin Salman, may his soul rest in peace.*

Each man, however long he lives
Must sometime make the ground his home

Death pursues us all
The noble, the free, must endure

Alas . . . of life and what it yields
I wish my heart knew naught

News reached me of this pain and
Prevented, tears, my eyes from sleep

The highest mountain cannot defeat him
The fiercest gale can never sway him

Spent, oh Salman, a night exhausted
From grief for our brother, departed

A command, and whatever God for us ordains
We accept, no matter what occurs

Ahmed, the noble, of whom we are proud
In Allah's care can never lose

And you, his father, of noble birth
Your home in the land long established

For you, condolences from hearts tormented
And for Fahad and his brothers, lions of Sharah*

*Sharah: A mountainous region in the Arabian Peninsula where the fiercest
lions are said to live; it means plentiful, generous.

SWORDS OF BEAUTY

Ease the ardor of my yearning, my lady
Reunite me with your vision

Erase the lines written by my tears
And with the ink of your kohled eye draw me

Oh, my life that sweetens my life
Oh, my hope for years remaining

Who gathered the winds for me and returned
The brightest years that slipped from my hands

Oh swords of beauty in eyes of oryx
You have so much – out of kindness give

The love from ever-sleepless eyes has faded
And my destiny, certain, this craving between us

Have mercy on the withered boughs
For love between lovers never dies

My love I proclaimed from peaks of highest mountains
Where, sadly, only echoes replied

With burning passion, only her name on my lips
Her I recall, and forget the existence of others

Heartbreaking my laments, yet neglected my grief
Though my words stir tears in the hardest hearts

Overwhelmed me, deep, bleeding wounds
Oh, oryx, from the pain of your wounds heal me

Leave me not with this fire – these regrets
Compassion and sympathy be yours – love is mine

AHMED RASHID THANI is an Emirati poet born in Khorfakkan in 1963. In 1981, he published a collection of poetry in vernacular Arabic. He republished it in the 1990s with additional poems, under the title *O! You Eat Dates . . . You Collect Gold*. This was followed by further volumes, including *Drowning Verge*, *Morning Sits Next to Sea*, and *Then Night Comes and Takes Me*. Thani's poems have been published in local and other Arab newspapers and magazines, and have been translated into French and German. He has participated in several celebrations and festivals of poetry in the UAE and the Arab world.

ON THE TABLE
Translated by Issa J. Boullata

I found everything in the closet
was threadbare
The torn school shirts,
The sex undergarments, and
The thinking cap.

Moss swims in the mirror's
swamp
And life's window is shut tight.
I opened a door I did not exit
from
I set a chair inside me
and waited for the impossible

On the table a book without first pages
Near the bottle words run
With no waves.

The day's candle is about to
be extinguished
In this barren room,
Under this dead ceiling

VALLEYS

Translated by Issa J. Boullata

Old valleys almost divulge
the secrets that waves break
against their foundations,
valleys imagine the cloud
with its fat and flesh
as it eats from the storms,
and other valleys that don't know
from where God brings
all this firewood.

The wave stopped laughing, for pain
fell into the sea.

KHULOOD AL MU'ALLA was born in Umm Al Quwain. She moved to Ras Al Khaimah in her childhood and completed her education there before attending United Arab Emirates University for her Bachelor's degree in Architecture. She went on to obtain a Master's degree in Project Management from Reading University in the UK and a Bachelor's degree in Arabic Language from Beirut University. She has published four volumes of poetry: *Here, I Lost the Time* (1997); *You, Alone* (1999); *Ha' of the Absent* (2003); and *Perhaps Here* (2008). In 2008, Khulood won the Buland Al Haidari Award for Young Arab Poets at the thirtieth Aseela International Cultural Festival in Morocco, an event that celebrates visionary poets and intellectuals from the Arab world.

BODY'S WINTER

Translated by Samia Touati, with Khulood Al Mu'alla

The sun pierces every detail
nothing casts a shadow
everything is burning
and this body is still cold.

AN UNEXCEPTIONAL POET
Translated by Samia Touati, with Khulood Al Mu'alla

I feel nothing
My poems are amassed
in drawers I have not opened for ages
I am a poet, who long keeps silent,
and does not shine at talk
When I speak from my heart
poems burst from my mouth,
like bodies burning with desire
but now, I sit considerably
I do not feel the parts of me
alienated from my body
I deemed myself with more depth
with more desire
I thought I was the one who creates the dreams of passersby
drawing close to the impossible
I was living my fullest glow
But now, I am alone
sitting on the coach of life
exposed
and the winter is unlike itself
my windows brace against the wind
I open my eyes that have long been closed
by kisses the sea sends
The sea has altered its seashores.
Now, here I am, alone
trying to hide my new poems in drawers with no keys
I long sit alone

no space for anything in me
and nothing is in the space
except for the shallow
poems of an unexceptional poet.

THE LANGUAGE OF THE SEA
Translated by Camilo Gómez-Rivas

I want to understand the language of the sea
to sleep long
between the falling and the rising.

INCESSANT PAIN
Translated by Camilo Gómez-Rivas

Every time a tear drops in the memory
the heart feels pain
fearing
what will fall tomorrow.

EGG
Translated by Camilo Gómez-Rivas

Love multiplies from the luminous house
the one with the windows opening out onto the sea
and I live inside an egg
and wait for love.

AMAL KHALID SULTAN AL QASSEMI, known also by the pseudonym Maysoon Al Khaledi, received a Bachelor's degree in Arabic Literature and Islamic Studies in 1987 from United Arab Emirates University. Since 2000, she has been Associate Dean for Community Affairs and Public Relations at the Higher Colleges of Technology, Sharjah, UAE. She served as a supervisor at the Technical Office of the General Deputy, Dubai from 1994 to 1999 and as an administrative supervisor from 1979 to 1983 at the Ministry of Education, Schools of Sharjah. She has contributed regular columns to several newspapers, including *Al Ittihad* from 1994 to 1999 and *Al Khaleej* from 2004 to the present. Her poems, short stories, and essays have appeared in those newspapers and in publications such as *Shurooq Journal*. She has participated in several international conferences, among them the Women's World Conference on Leadership, Boston, US in 2007.

FOUR LEAVES OF BASIL

Translated by Bahaa-eddin M. Mazid

No trace of me
in the Book of Joy;
nor a letter so barren
in the alphabet of sadness.
The white thorns
on which my feet have trodden
never brought good news at all.
Nor has the black
shrouding me
like death.
The howling wind
has never been
a sign of waste.
Nor has the rain of happiness

poured a drink
in my cup.
I have never cried
for being unfairly treated,
my fate endangered
by oppression, and me
drinking woe.
Never have I laughed of joy
while clouds danced at my door.
I have come back
crying from the womb
of humility and oppression
to the night cooing
my pain.
The dawn is just a mirage
and I wander lonely
and without aim
until I am worn out
and fatigued.
I have knocked at doors
of fortunetellers,
wandered in the valley of *jinnis*
believed in magic
and superstitions
and the echoing of winds
in my heart.
I made my offerings
and burned incense
for your homecoming.
I came back to live
the rest of my disappointment.
Springs of sadness
overflowed from me
while joy remained
imprisoned inside.

I have never knocked at your door
seeking something I need;
I have always been happy
with the little I have.
You were the cloud
protecting me,
while I was hellfire
for you.
You were my rain,
pure and flowing,
while I was your waste,
your burning torture.
I had nothing to do
with rain
when you whispered—
Here is the night
washed in rain,
delighted in my letter
and in yours
in my voice and in yours
in my sadness and in yours
in my illusion and in yours.
We are strangers
lost in the valley
of sadness,
with wounds
regenerating.
On our calendars,
we turn pages of misery,
now and then
recall the past
and choke
with moans.
Here is the history
of long absence

and here is my story
of departure
and of oppression.
My wounds are timeless
so that there is no last time.
My horses and yours have raced
on the horizon of sadness.
When you stumbled
I whined loudly
and back I went
begging you
to carry on.
I walk alone,
as lonely as I have always been
since my birth
guided by the star that I call you,
holding fast to four
leaves of basil—
one for when I am sick
of sadness;
another when I choke
with tears
and with yearning and pain;
the third when in the darkness
of my lonely soul
I need company;
and the last one,
wheat for my dark grave,
in the hopes that I will see
you again in the afterlife.

ANWAR ALKHATIB of the United Arab Emirates was born in Lebanon in 1954. He earned his BA in Foreign Languages, with English as his major, from the University of Constantin in Algeria in 1976. He has worked as an editor and journalist for *Al Ittihad* newspaper in Abu Dhabi for thirteen years and at the Higher Colleges of Technology in the Emirates for seven years. He currently works at the Ministry of Presidential Affairs in Abu Dhabi, a position he has held for three years. He has published seventeen books, including ten novels, three collections of short fiction, two collections of poetry, and two books of literary criticism.

No Land for Passersby

Translated by Allison Blecker

O Princess of Mirage
Don't search for glory in the train of the displaced
Don't confide in the land beneath them
There is no land for passersby
no carrier pigeons, or library
In torn notebooks
with mended lines they write their poems
and memories with which they burden the wind
Don't search for desire in their eyes
There is no room for longing
Everyone carries his mother,
his father's will,
his lover's handkerchief
and a bit of nostalgia
There is no land for passersby
Don't search for them on airport runways
They are disturbed by Immigration and Customs

They choke and despair before the names
on the houses
They avert their eyes from the gathering of families in parks
Tales of fires captivate them
They mock flags
and walk alone,
their features fade in the crowd
Some are departing and others are left behind
In memory of defeats
Every day, they write:
We are returning . . .
Then they drink until drunk . . .

TWO GATES TO REDEMPTION

Translated by Allison Blecker

❧

The sea has two gates to insomnia
One leads to unknown ports,
the other to drowning
I will choose redemption
Thus, the fortuneteller of twilight compelled me
and buried the color of water in the sunset of my eyes
She filled holes in my soul with sand
and drew a torn sail on my forehead
On the horizon memory burned
and there was a corpse stretched out on a boat
that belonged to sailors returned from ports unknown
To make a choice, two questions:
Will I be redeemed if the waves cast me
upon shores inconstant as beautiful women?
Will I be redeemed if I live in a kingdom of slumber?
The fortuneteller said in a bewildered voice:
"Put your alphabet to the test . . .
Ports unknown to you don't mean you're lost
and your labyrinthine wandering in the depths doesn't mean death"
If I strike the sea with my staff it might split . . .
Or a friendly whale might take me to a foreign land
The truth has one face: I am not a prophet
or the founder of a doctrine
I don't claim to walk on water
All my wishes are the size of a sparrow
in the crown of a cypress tree
From it, I survey the horizon
for an idea that has not been suffocated.
I stand before the narrowing waters

and embrace the meaning of a life without banks
On a road of water, I draw a fork for every two waves
A third wave scatters after gathering into a sphere that doesn't last
For a second time I draw on her breasts a pair of sea gulls
flying after a fourth wave
I draw a fork, then a seventh wave
then another
arriving at a wave in the making
The truth has half a face: I am not a sorcerer
nor do I possess a drop that moistens an illusion
which ages and departs
The fortuneteller told me: "Don't put your heart to the test in
the water"
But I forgot
She said: "When your visions exhaust you, trespass upon my
isolation"
But I forgot
Then when I bared my chest
The teller of basil did not write the address of my solitude
I remained defenseless, sewing a carpet from sea foam
that broke, scattered and then sighed
I didn't sigh
I was in need of the sea's breasts
To feed me a bit of the ports' milk
The truth has many faces: my mother can't bear the sea
She was busy untangling the map of my dead
Pictures drawn in the void burdened me,
the spouts of my sorrow opened
and I began to gather my waves from the sea
so they would not get mixed
A child hastening toward his mother passed by me
He faced the two gates of the sea
I said to him: "On the horizon, there are two gates
One leads to your mother's soul,

the other to two forks"
He chose to draw a sea on the sea
and travel far from the two gates

WHEN WE GROW OLDER
Translated by Allison Blecker

When we grow older
we begin to observe the boring details of life:
The arrival of night faster than the day expects
The arrival of day slower than the night anticipates
Appointment-free mornings
The boredom of coffee with its smidgen of sugar
spilling over into its saucer
The sameness of flavors in food
The sameness of places
Our hatred of mirrors
Our indifference to the girls passing by
The sameness of all our limbs
When we grow older
we begin to suffer from a paucity of expectations:
We don't expect a visitor, a relative, a beloved
nor a phone call from an old friend
We don't expect news
victory, nor defeat
For all that was going to happen has already come to pass
We don't expect anything
We don't expect that we will expect anything
Except what we already know and reject
Except that someone will inform us
we were found in the road, disoriented
or lost, or moving toward an idea unknown to us
which we know well
When we grow older we don't wait for anyone
For the arrival of winter is a quandary,
the arrival of summer is a heavy burden
and the autumn leaves resemble us . . . and terrify us

All our waiting is for self-evident things:
Our sleeplessness in the totality of our breaths
Our ability to recall who is around us
The deeds to our land
The locations of our house keys
The ambush sites that count us
and rejoice when the crowd in our houses diminishes
When we grow older, we understand what it means that
we have grown older
and those who lie in wait don't understand
that whenever we grow older
they grow younger in our eyes

MAISOON SAQR AL QASIMI, born in Abu Dhabi, UAE is a poet and painter. She received her Master's degree in Economics and Political Science from Cairo University in 1981. From 1989 to 1995, she was Director of the Department of Culture in the UAE Ministry of Information and Culture. She has published ten collections of poetry and has held solo exhibitions in Tunisia, Bahrain, Egypt, the UAE, and Paris. She has participated in group exhibitions in Washington, DC, Amman, Jordan, and Abu Dhabi. She lives in Cairo and Abu Dhabi.

A MAD MAN WHO DOES NOT LOVE ME
Translated by Khaled Mattawa

I am of you.
You raise me with your means,
and my spirit is steadfast in its love.
Because of it I remain clinging to delusions,
and in the shade I search for a twin
to pair it with what has settled in the depths
of this body's desire.
But which body is it?

I hear music calling you.
Your heart is wide enough to house me.
As soon as I move further
I only become a woman
who is not content with the blame that lights her shade.
I was never yours before,
but even in space I do move about
dispersing my being.

The fickle pace of the days grinds on
and nothing settles except what peers from our windows.
It gains strength with the wind that carries it on its back and spins it.
And so the days have spun us too.
Will you turn your head a bit to the back?
Do you recall me
then hold my hand and guide it toward farewell?
I will not be alone,
and you will not be – after this – alone.

The river of my affection rolls on,
its tributaries are countless.
Will it quench your thirst
to walk further into your question?
I become the daughter of an un-lived time
whenever I open the door for the word,
and daughter of this night that muffles your secrets
which I hold so that you would not reveal them.
If you'd uttered them, your longings would have scattered along
the horizon.
But no horizon will save you from this disbursement,
and no death after the death that has wound our hearts together.
How will we abbreviate the nations and the histories within us?
I remain a stranger to you, I know,
but closer than this blood that throbs in your veins.

I collapse into loss.
I say: I will move on.
Will you care for this sapling that wakes beside you?
Will you proceed through love toward it?
Which is your favorite, the henna flower or the lemon blossom,
the soul that is of you,
or am I born in the wink of your lips as they say "I love you"?
Have you said such a thing,
or do I hear it in dream?

I dance on a hand span of earth.
It will suffice me if ever I held this word
that leaps from lips toward the heart
and sleeps like a sparrow in the nest of its birth.
I long for your hands,
two doves that shade the blaze of my longing.
Do you too miss me, or do you not remember
the particulars of my voice?

I say: we have one outlet, no more,
from this confusion, toward the sadness
of this love that has dropped us in its abyss,
toward this wide earth that is too narrow for us,
toward the soul in which we mirror each other, toward that shape.
We go on into the question
like a cloud that rains whenever the winds tempt it.
What wind can bind us,
and why do we enact our insistence on parting?
Maybe our cruelty has ripened
and now our wish for rupture has overpowered us.
Maybe our worries have returned again.
How do we muffle our love,
and how can I hear your voice in this world
when I hear nothing but it?
You, who've fed me the bread of your love,
I've sought refuge from you.
I said: kill it inside you and save yourself?
But have I spared myself one solitude
only to live another where my language is shattered.

How did this fruit ripen so?
My questions are in the sea.
You arrive and I leave.
You reveal nothing and I talk too much.
I spend the day touching events as they pass.
I speak to see myself.

Travel is hung on a hook.
The seller of lies is on his daily tour.
We walk behind him with our stories
to keep busy,
to acquire a calm mood
without profound questions or fruit,
without a heart that beats, not even once.

Like pebbles on the road,
they tread upon us and we remain,
stones that listen well
and roll along.
Time is in their hands,
and in us constant dreams
and images of that fruit.

Don't turn around.
I insist on walking behind you.
I adorn myself and I become,
always heading in an opposite direction.
This is how I will betray my love.
I will say: history moves me
so that I immortalize my mouth in the motions of weeping,
my hand in the saying goodbye.
There is a sky turbulent with love.

I saw you.
I said: I see you with my heart.
My heart is the piece of flesh that beats,
and my eyes only pile images . . .
I said: I'll be lying if I fled.
How will I move through space alone?
My hand will not lead me toward it.
It can't.
There's a turbulent sky
and nature is condemned because of me.

I said: there's a lightness to you that flows
with the water I call "affection."
I see you
and I am quickly defeated
whenever what I expect falls in my lap.

In daytime, the sadness of solitude leaves me.
At night, I fly with the wings of my dreams
hoping there is no end.
I, who love to lose quickly,
sometimes fever shakes me so that I waken,
so that I am not defeated,
so that I do not sleep stricken with delusions
afraid of a turn that will break my bones.
And with the ribs of love I make ropes
and climb.
As if I am balling up words and throwing them through a little hole...
And like a syringe shot into bone
that enters with a tiny puncture,
a quick surgery on emotions,
you drag my losses with you, and go.
You said: you're not mine.
I seek your face in the blood of genealogies.
I said: you don't love me.

And nothing remains in the body
except this wan soul of mine.

I leave my hand held in your hands.
Time takes me away.
I disappear
still holding on to your hands.
I move on
and my hand remains in yours.
I sleep my last sleep, handless,
and you are a lonely man,
a man for coincidences,
a spectator at this circus,
a blind man watching blackness.

I will not exchange my body for a shadow
that traverses a nearby sky.
I will not leave the place,
because the place is the essence of pain.

When you pass before me
my shadow seeps through you.
My reflection, shadowed by my affection
hovers over your euphoria,
but you still don't love me.

You hear me
and your ear is tuned to the street.
You see me
and neither of your eyes have vision.
I speak
and you smile innocently and with joy.
Whenever I believe my intuitions
all this becomes a labyrinth,
and whenever I chase cats

they exchange lives.
I should just smile
and nod,
and when you speak normally
I should just discharge my delusions and leave.

What's a dream really worth?
Losses come
and I stand before them
paralyzed or contemplative
waiting beside my body.

I walk wearing soft sandals
to awaken my feet with slow strides.
My face in love,
I toss it around like a piece of clothing,
sweat smeared or steaming with sadness.
You explode my longings in the mirror,
and so I smile—
the air in my heart breezes,
and with a shot from a small camera
and with a lens that concentrates light on our condition
you process it all in our last picture
which only shows our shadows.

But today you're a lover
without cruelty,
and your voice
does not reveal my discovery of you.
You were in a book,
and now you've become my legend.
I walk in the rain;
I talk to myself.
Each night is a dagger,
each forest is in the breast.

My life is a melody in my ear,
a desire drenched with light.
This whole world is just a thought.
The past is a rhythm we can neither proceed through
nor that can save us.

We must make this connection.
You must get used to taking me from the depths.
Under the tree
you read all my news,
you drank them with my voice.
Under the tree
you kissed my hand and studied it at the doorstep.
You held it to pull me toward you.
But you don't love me.

I said: he'll disappear one day,
and he will not know where my road is taking him.
I am the tree not the fruit.
How can we name the goal quickly
when we don't trust the motions of time?
I said: he really doesn't understand me,
his eyes are adrift,
his heart tucked away, hidden,
and he doesn't understand me
and doesn't want to.

I revealed my longings,
I left them at the doorstep.
I said: he'll take me away,
but he preferred to sit on a chair
in a garden
under a tree
watching the days
and slitting them with his razor.

He doesn't want my attention,
doesn't want my testaments of love.
He doesn't want my obvious weakness,
and doesn't want my strength.
I always miscalculate
and he doesn't want my miscalculations.

Could it be that we're that different,
or has the humidity of our sentiments
seeped through us so thoroughly
and killed our spirits?

I think of making things better,
our bond waning from boredom,
our flame that has gone early to bed,
and the affection that has collapsed on the carpet of days . . .
How do we bring them back?

I'm often wrong when I suspend my confidence in the air
for it falls,
and my blood falls with it
and sorrows come at me multiplied.
I'm wrong when I'm naked like this,
like a marble statue
revealing all my dreams and tears,
revealing all my love,
embracing my one body
with its veins and arteries,
careless about my nerves.
And the one nerve cell that I care for,
you leave it behind in the room
by the window
and go.

Every day
from a flutter in a sparrow's wing
to the euphoria of desire in eyes,
to smiles on lips,
to a shiver in a hand,
we arrive again
and again at the same loneliness.

What would happen
if you had looked with a more discerning eye,
if you stretched your soul toward the woodening of mine,
if you brushed my forehead a little
and lay down beside me?

A butterfly
with a fallen wing
can easily break your longing.
And I can exchange my soul
for a thread flowing evenly at the edge of sleep . . .

On a landing strip and under a sky
that rains mercilessly on my body . . .
on my eternally ready body that awaits a cloud to drop
all its water
while I'm dressed for a soirée.
I go back home drenched
without going where I'd intended.

I exchange my femininity
with a light walk in gentleness,
I swallow a great deal of stupidity
before speaking.
You give me your hand
and we speak like foes.
I say: I deserve to be loved more.

A woman who loves you,
you deserve to love her more.

Each day I drop a feather
from my wings
into your cradle.
You did not gather them into a wing,
I could not get to your heart.
I'd thought you were the prince on the white horse
chasing colorful butterflies.
I thought you were a panther extinguishing his daylight with night.

The time that runs,
you too are in it,
and the years that passed before you
are not distant.
Time is wrinkles on the face.
You can't extinguish it.
You are the shadow of that stubborn face.
What shall I do now?
I'll eat tomorrow's pancakes,
take sleeping pills,
wake to the dreams that have devoured me,
and begin with an optimistic step on the road.

Those who desire me will send me packing to your heart.
You will delight in hearing my cries in the wilderness.
You should have waited for me.
A thousand hands are ready to catch me,
but I have become a tree and my hands are its leaves.
Fruit falls ripe from me,
even rotten,
and I am the tree not the fruit
for I have dug into the sand
and filled my mouth with grass.

If it weren't for the roofs that edge my apprehensions,
if you'd waited for the wet clothes to dry on a rope
that can withstand water's descent back to earth.
if you, love, were that angel that fluttered on my shoulders
when I turned,
I would have been with him,
and you would have been closer . . .

You return me to oblivion
with an impediment of wisdom,
and I strut on
as you call out to me.
O love,
you are beyond emotion's reach,
and we are here.
Regret is pelting the walls.
We shouldn't disintegrate here,
we shouldn't enter the maze
delighting in pain,
carrying the chance of being borne out to the world
while the soul's shell remains shut firm with its secrets.

A mad man
who does not love me,
who doesn't care
about my melting.
I am the tree
not the fruit.
As long as he keeps his vision from seeing,
I will not lead him with a candle in hand.

The difference between the distances I know
and the reaches of my soul, is a wide horizon.
I push the parameters further apart
so that all my distances are evened out
and not crowded out by the small details . . .

It's as if we know the size of the loss . . .
The man who doesn't love me,
his visage has changed with time,
but my tenderness, my source of pride,
will find its place in a heart
that won't retrieve all the decay in affection.
It will never return as long as my longing is impossible to shake.

His upper hand
was strong and giving,
shepherding love.
It still presses with its cruelty
while I, constantly anxious,
live on the lower tiers
to protect myself from the terror of falling
from his windows that lean downward
toward a merciless stone ground.
Except for a word
said with extreme frugality,
I never heard a thing.

I am not used to the caress of praise.
I never let history walk into the present.
Yet when I submerge myself in this cruelty
which I exaggeratingly call "love,"
it begins to shape the malady that devours me,
the onset of paralysis.

You are cruel and I respond.
This is not a weakness,
rather a greater persistence of the same cruelty.
You are cruel so that I weep.
But my weeping is not cowering.
I merely let the present walk into the future and I do not find
you there.
You are cruel and you leave,

and I am here
facing the absence that my failure has made.
You are cruel and I am cruel.
The difference is still great.
It's to defend what love I carry within me.
You are cruel and I disappear
so that I maintain a little of myself,
so that I can.

HOW LUCKY THE FISHERMAN IS
Translated by Allison Blecker

○⁊○

Did one of them picture me?
O drowning, did you defeat me?
You burdened me with more than I could bear,
and slackened the rope on the ship's mast.
O sea, I was your pearl,
then you cast me into the fisherman's hand.
When he handed me to the captain
I raged and revolted.
O sea, did you defeat him
when you snatched me from him
so I fell, slipping from the oyster
into your depths
beside his drowned corpse
that still clutched
the empty oyster?
Did you lower your eyes
while the fish swallowed me?
Did watch as the net ensnared me?
Did you know I was in the fish's stomach,
and when I entered the house
they gathered for the meal and ate it,
and I fell into the mouth of a young girl?
She placed me in a rough hand,
I recognized his rough hand,
I recognized it.
It is the same hand
that split me like an oyster
and bore me to the captain.
How lucky the fisherman is.

I AM THE ONLY CAT HERE
Translated by Allison Blecker

What do I say in the tent,
I with my seductive eyes?

I, whose poem meows
at the feet of poetry,
I am the only cat here
who licks her wounds
without complaint.
While the coffee boils over
in the tent.
I sit and paint the edges of my eyelids with kohl.
I tell myself
that I am a widow
when I puncture the paper
with the pen nib.
While I shape the kohl on my eyelids
with a pencil, I tell myself:
The dagger will pierce his heart,
his blood will explode onto my face,
I will drink it, toasting revenge.
I open my painted eyes and say:
I will learn evil,
I will learn how to be
the widow of a highway robber.

INSTEAD OF MIRRORS
Translated by Khaled Al Masri

Only one man
for her
for her body, hanging on, waiting
for a heart, sealed against her will,
and for these two hands trembling with desire,
two hands, like a nest without a bird or chicks,
and this soul, which dwindles and dwindles
like these fires.
A man shares with her loneliness and a bed,
giving her children instead of mirrors
and love instead of weeping, deep in her sleep.

THANI AL-SUWAIDI of the United Arab Emirates was born in 1966 in Ras al-Khayma. He has published two collections of poetry: *Liyajiff Riq al-Bahr* [So the Sea's Foam May Dry Out] (1991) and *al-Ashya' Tamurr* [Stuff Happens] (2000). His novella *al-Dizil* [The Diesel] was published in 1994 in Beirut, reprinted in Baghdad in 2006, and then published in 2008 in Cairo. He works as a journalist for the Emirates newspaper *Al Ittihad*.

A DAY

Translated by William M. Hutchins

It was a day
That seemed to have fallen from a star's prong.
I saw the fire reach out
Like a sleeper
Whose eyes are dazzled;
I saw three mendicants
Who became a single figure with two sticks
When I touched them.

It was a day
Of rain that halted halfway across the sky
And swore by a tree
That it wouldn't wet any child's head.
It was a day
When I saw the sea prowl through the city.
On resolving to return to his seabed,
He forgot a wave on my balcony.
After I had bathed in it for a year,
We both evaporated.

It was a day
When I apologized to my head,
Which I haven't encountered often,
But at which my friends used to aim coffee each evening,
Hitting it with a single shot
And then attaching it to my body,
Saying,
"What a worthless catch!"

DELUSION
Translated by Hart Uhl

My friends often reproached me
For my squandered years.
I often fancied that I believed them.
As for now,
All I can do
Is stare at my carpet.
I change its place
As if changing my life.

THE SHEPHERD
Translated by William M. Hutchins

Starting today
I'll hang my coat on the wind
And let it fly off
Like the scent of orange blossoms in the field,
Which is exceptionally lovely
When vipers and orange buds meet there.
What daredevil can
Spoil their delightful tryst?
What tempting tree can destroy their love?
The day they dug up the field
They found that the sod was mixed with the shepherd's blood,
That the wolf, savoring its delight, was departing,
And that the good people
Who dwell in the field,
Despising the darkness,
Were releasing vipers in their dreams.
Meanwhile the field's shepherd
Sat alone, remembering
His lambs and gazelles
Frolicking while he slept.
Every man on the lam has a moon that guides him to purity.

TESTAMENT
Translated by William M. Hutchins

I write out my will and fall asleep.
Soon
The rain pours down and
Blurs my testament.
In the morning
I wonder
Whether the rain has left you my body.

TRANSIENCE
Translated by Ghada Gherwash

When grass awoke from my blood
He was alone,
Heading for the garden,
The sand was dreaming then
About a woman's corpse looking out the window.
Dead people
Who have sold the earth . . . they leave
With mouths closed by a red tongue.
Darkness falls on them to melt the sun.
I will stay like this a long time:
Dead and alive.
Houses leave me wide open,
And the faces go cold as I die.
And when I die
Let my mother Fatima,
Hang my laundry on your roofs
And on my papers,
Write a story for the children of my country,
About the desert that fell in love with a tent.
Tell them
That every day he danced with the waves,
Fishing the sea with his eyes.
Tell them
That villagers covered him with their
Brown bread
And planes swept rapidly over his sorrow;
His eyes were vast shadows and his tongue was a silent king.

Ever since the wind first met the sky,
They have lived together, giving birth to him,
The grandchild of a tree.
His soul is a fruit,
And his body is the descendant of feathers.
Love is his big and last hope,
Whenever he feels delighted,
The morning starts dancing,
And whenever final pains glow;
He remembers the death of his fingers
At the end of the day.
He smells once more the coffee that created his head.
His rooms conspire against him
To prepare charming dreams.

Ever since he started talking slowly,
His own cries wouldn't believe him anymore,
And his life wouldn't think about him anymore.

His life is a paper that flies away on a strong wind.
Some of his days were doomed,
Others caused mountains to fall on cities.
With the reflection of the moon on the bed,
His illusions expand in the middle of the night.

⚬

When I die;
Break the sky
And distribute its stars to those who pass by,
And on my tombstone write:
Here is where the sand bathes the body of a poet.
Separate me from the soil of rogues,
And let the ants carry me
To where paradise lies.
Let me shake off catastrophe with a finger of regret.

Oh God,
Why is it only me who pulls trees by their hair?
Why do you embarrass me and accept all my mistakes.
And if all my gardens burn,
I see you still take care of my grass in the sea.

When I die
Let the women hold back;
Let me also cry before you do,
Because I made death out of a small house.
Let everything be small
Just like I was
There's one person who shouldn't visit my grave:
"me."

I am the one who is poured out with the river,
Who didn't love anybody
And whom no one loved.
He sits on a wayward cloud
To guide his reeling rain to the world
And whenever he catches a star
He astonishes his friends with his poetry.
That's who I am:
The grandchild of a tree
Who left his personal effects as a tip for the barman
And wandered aimlessly at birth,
Thinking of the purpose of his existence
And the purpose of his nonexistence;
He found death in his love
And in his body, he found the earth's dissolution.

POEMS FOR THE WIND
Translated by Joseph T. Zeidan

1

Because I am solitary
Or perhaps conceited
I go out with the walls in my hand
As if the house carries me around
As if the streets speak
In the language of the house
As if the creatures are keys
So I can go back once again
And open my house

2

The soul is a servant to the body
The soul fears the dirt
And hides in a jar with holes
Therefore the body always yearns
For the house with a big window

3

A year in which I was born and finished
And in the other
I took the previous year
And stopped the descending of years
So that I may not be finished

4

Run away
The thieves are advancing toward the rivulet
Carry me with you
My legs reached the end
And my soul the beginning

5

The cloud is the crossroad of the rain
Rain is a tear from a sad cloud
I am wet this evening
Wet by a cold winter
Where the bars spread out their glasses
Under my eyes
Where I warm myself up
With what does not interest me

KHALID ALBUDOOR was born in Dubai. He studied mass communication at the University of the United Arab Emirates and then attended Ohio University in the US for his MA in Scriptwriting. He began publishing his poetry in 1980 and has been active in his community, helping to establish the Emirati Writers' Union and participating in several poetry reading nights and film festivals in the UAE and abroad. Since 1989, he has worked as a radio and television program writer and presenter and has also produced several documentary films and programs. He was the director of Radio Dubai from 2000 to 2005. He is now a researcher, consultant, and writer on UAE history and cultural heritage, and serves as UAE representative to the International Organization of Folk Art. Albudoor, who won the Al Kha Prize for Poetry in Lebanon in 1991, has published five poetry collections and has written extensively for local and other Arab publications.

EVERYTHING

Everything is in place
Your mirror
Your gem stones
The burning oil pot
The henna pot
For the *Eid** to come.
An empty chair
Last summer's shirt
Your scent on the pillow
Remnants of our last day's kiss
Everything is there
Even the sun
We saw sinking behind our balcony
Everything, but you

*Eid is a holy day for Muslims.

LANTERN

The moon stays
All night
Hanging like a lantern
In the dark
I am looking at patches of silver clouds
That enveloped the moon
Searching for a dream
I lost
When I was a small boy.

SOON

∽

We will meet soon
But we will soon part again
Not knowing the next meeting place.

It is two seasons since we last met
Your hair is long now
The last time
We built a house of words.

When I imagined you
Watering the plants on the balcony
You were reading leaves
I know
That this moment is short
This embrace and
Our lives, together and apart
Too soon swept away
By winds of disappearances.

But for now, we will meet
And I will let you rest
Like a soft shadow
On my arm.

All That We Have

Because there is no one there
Now is the time
For me
To set off
On the road
Toward the desert.
There
I will be
Where no one covers the horizon
Or prevents the sky from falling
On my head.
When the winter comes
Or the summer nears
With its burning winds
I would be the wanderer
Who's searching
For you.
The night
Binds me like a page in a book
And when the morning surprises me
With its sun,
The red apple,
I will stand
Like an old monastery's column
Uttering melodies
Of traveling Bedouins,
Praying for the darkness
With all my heart's beats
So my voice can
Reach you.

It will not be too late
In the age
To come back to you
Because your voice always comes back
And burns my life
With your hot breath.

I see an image of your body
Lying in the dark
Burning
And I ask
How can we learn love
When night is dry
Like an old tree
And all the horizons
Are not welcoming
For the journey.

I extend my hand
But cannot touch you
I know
We are two souls
In solitude
I know daydreams
Are all that we have
When our hearts search
For shelter.

I approach wells in the summer
I find that
You are the water,
And in winter nights
You are burning with enigmatic light
Your lightning breaks the sky,
For that

My dream's desert
Is bright.

Because no one is there
We will lie down
On the shoulder of a dune
Gazing silently
At colors of far hills
We wait for no one
You might say
No more Bedouins
They disappeared
All of them
Before we knew them
Or wrote their names
On the skins of our tent
Before we learned love from them
And I would say
Look carefully
Behind our dune
I can see their souls approach us
Rising from the mirage of distance
Or
Appearing to us from
The future.

I extend my hand
Toward you
Carrying a few daydreams
This
Is all that remains for us.
And we have a few more years
To build our tent
Near the wells,
We will stay all night

With the light of
Our existence
While we wait for the Bedouins
To stop their journeys
To settle into the sand
We will hand them buckets
Filled with water
And they, from their time worn bags,
Will hand us
Love
So we can learn it
Again.

THE TRANSLATORS

൙

Ruanne Abou-Rahme is a Palestinian artist and filmmaker. She is the director of *Double Exposure* (2008), a documentary "inspired by the immediate need to express the new realities a generation of young Palestinians face."

Hend Mubarek Aleidan of Doha, Qatar is a 2009 graduate of Virginia Commonwealth University in Qatar, holding a BFA in Graphic Design. Her initial work on *Gathering the Tide* came under the auspices of an Undergraduate Research Experience Program grant awarded by the Qatar Foundation and the Qatar National Research Fund.

Abdulla Al-Harrasi holds a PhD in Translation Studies from Aston University, UK, specializing in Metaphor in Arabic-into-English Translation. He was an assistant professor in the College of Arts at Sultan Qaboos University before becoming head of the Omani Encyclopedia Project. He is a member of the European Society of Translation Studies.

Laith al-Husain is a translator of poetry and prose and a specialist in comparative literature.

Salma Khadra Al Jayyusi obtained her PhD in 1970 from the School of Oriental and African Studies, London University, UK, specializing in Arabic literature, following earlier studies at the American University of Beirut. She is known as a scholar, translator, anthologist, analyst, and disseminator of Arabic literature, both classic and contemporary, and is the author of the seminal 1992 book *Anthology of Modern Palestinian Literature*.

Khaled Al-Masri obtained his PhD in Near Eastern Studies from the University of Michigan, Ann Arbor and his MA and BA in Arabic Language and Literature from Yarmouk University in Irbid, Jordan. He joined Harvard University, US in Fall 2005 as a preceptor of Arabic. He has published in Arabic a book on the fiction of prominent Iraqi author Gha'ib Tu'mah Faraman. Additionally, he has edited several Arabic translations of

English novels, including *Housekeeping*, *Gilead*, and *Home* by Marilynne Robinson and *The Known World* by Edward P. Jones. He is the editor and co-translator of a forthcoming anthology of Arabic short stories to be published by Penguin.

Hameed Al Qaed, born in Bahrain in 1948, is a poet, writer, and translator. He has published three collections of poetry, In 2007, he compiled and translated *Pearl, Dreams of Shell* (Howling Dog Press, US), a collection of work from twenty-nine contemporary Bahraini poets. He has published extensively in Arabic newspapers, magazines, and periodicals, and has participated in many poetry readings and conferences in Bahrain and overseas.

Sara Al Qatami of Doha, Qatar is a student pursuing a BFA in Graphic Design in the class of 2012 at Virginia Commonwealth University in Qatar. Her initial work on *Gathering the Tide* came under the auspices of an Undergraduate Research Experience Program grant awarded by the Qatar Foundation and the Qatar National Research Fund.

Haifa Al Sanousi has a PhD in Modern Arabic Literature from the University of Glasgow and is an associate professor of Arabic literature at Kuwait University. Al Sanousi has published extensively in the field of literary criticism and is the author of several collections of short stories, novellas, children's books, and training manuals for literature and therapeutic healing workshops.

Salih J. Altoma, born in Iraq, received his BA from the University of Baghdad and his MAT and EdD from Harvard University, US. He has published works in Arabic and English on modern Arabic literature and on Arab and western literary relations, including *Modern Arabic Poetry in English Translation: A Bibliography* and *Modern Arabic Literature in Translation: A Companion*. He is Professor Emeritus of Arabic and Comparative Literature at Indiana University, US, having served as its director of Middle Eastern Studies and chair of its Department of Near Eastern Languages and Cultures.

Allison Blecker received her BA in Middle Eastern Studies and Politics from New York University and her MA in Middle Eastern Studies from Harvard University. She is currently a doctoral student at Harvard University in the Department of Near Eastern Languages and Civilizations studying Arabic literature.

Issa J. Boullata was born in Jerusalem and received his PhD in Arabic Literature from London University, UK in 1969. His numerous publications include *Modern Arab Poets, 1950–1975*; *Badr Shakir al-Sayyab: His Life and Poetry*; and translations of contemporary Arab authors such as Mohamed Berrada, Emily Nasrallah, and Ghada Samman. His translation of Jabra Ibrahim Jabra's *The First Well: A Bethlehem Boyhood* won the inaugural Arabic Translation Award sponsored by the King Fahd Center at the University of Arkansas and the University of Arkansas Press. His most recent academic position has been as professor of Arabic literature at the Institute of Islamic Studies of McGill University in Montreal, Canada.

Sargon Boulus was an Iraqi Assyrian poet and short story writer. He studied comparative literature at the University of California at Berkeley and sculpture at Skyline College. His poetry has been published in major Arab magazines. His English-to-Arabic translations include work by W. S. Merwin, Allen Ginsberg, Gary Snyder, Michael McClure, and others.

Alan Brownjohn is a British poet and novelist, educated at Merton College, Oxford, UK. He has been a regular broadcaster, reviewer, and contributor to journals such as the *Times Literary Supplement*, *Encounter*, and the *Sunday Times*, poetry critic for the *New Statesman*, and chairman of the Poetry Society. His first collection of poetry, *The Railings*, was published in 1961. Other collections include *Collected Poems 1952–1983* (1983) and *The Observation Car* (1990). He is also the author of four novels, two books for children, and a critical study of the poet Philip Larkin.

Patricia Alanah Byrne is an American poet and literary editor who lives in Massachusetts. She has taught literature and writing at Wellesley School and has published three books of poetry.

Jinan M. Coulter is a video artist with degrees from Royal Holloway College, University of London, the London College of Printing, and Goldsmiths College, University of London.

Anne Fairbairn is an Australian poet and journalist. In 1998, she received the Order of Australia for services to literature and international relations between Australia and the Middle East.

Shihab Ghanem of Dubai is an engineer, a manager, an economist, a poet, and a translator of poetry from Arabic to English and vice versa. He has published thirty books, including eight books of poetry in Arabic and one in English, and several volumes of translated poetry, from Arabic to English and from Malayalam and other languages to Arabic via English.

Ghada Gherwash is originally from Tripoli, Libya. A poet and teacher, in 2006 she moved to the US to teach Arabic as a Fulbright Teaching Fellow at Appalachian State University in Boone, North Carolina, where she also obtained her MA in English.

Camilo Gómez-Rivas is an assistant professor of Middle Eastern History in the Department of Arab and Islamic Civilizations, American University in Cairo.

Nay Hannawi was born and raised in southern Lebanon and received her BA in English from American University in Beirut. She has taught Arabic and English at the University of Arkansas, US, where she received her MFA in Literary Translation. In July 1999, her translation of Jabbour Douaihy's *Autumn Equinox* won the Arkansas Prize for Literary Translation from Arabic. She now works as a translator in Kuwait and teaches English at Kuwait University.

Mohammed Ali Harfouch translated Souad Al-Mubarak Al-Sabah's "Love Poem 1".

Joseph Heithaus is chair of the English Department at DePauw University, US. He recently co-wrote *Rivers, Rails, and Runways* with a group of Indiana poets who have had their poems etched into the glass murals of artist Martin Donlin at the Indianapolis International Airport. His poems have appeared in a number of literary journals, including *New York Quarterly*, *The Southern Review*, and *Poetry*.

William M. Hutchins is Professor of Philosophy and Religion at Appalachian State University, US. Among his translations are Mohammed al-Khudayyir's *Basrayatha: Portrait of a City*, Fadhil al-Azzawi's *The Last of The Angels*, Ibrahim al-Koni's *Anubis*, and Ibrahim al-Mazini's *Ten Again*. He is also the principal translator of Nobel laureate Naguib Mahfouz's *Cairo Trilogy* and the sole translator of Mahfouz's *Cairo Modern*. In 2005–2006, he was awarded a US National Endowment for the Arts

Literary Translation Grant for the translation of *The Seven Veils of Seth* by
Ibrahim al-Koni.

Lena Jayyusi is associate professor and graduate program coordinator of
the College of Communication and Media Sciences at Zayed University's
Dubai Campus. She has published work on the role of Palestinian broadcast-
ing, the Palestinian media during the Oslo peace process, the globalization
of human rights discourse, and the role of media in democracy.

Amira Kashgary is an assistant professor of linguistics in the Department
of English, College of Education at King Abdulaziz University in Jeddah,
Saudi Arabia. She holds two Master's degrees from Stanford University,
US and a doctorate from King Abdulaziz University, Saudi Arabia.

Hafiz Kheir, a graduate of the Film and Television School at the London
Institute, is a writer, translator, and filmmaker. Originally from Sudan, he
now lives in the UK.

Heather Lawton collaborated with A. A. Ruffai and Saudi poet Ghazi Al
Ghosaibi to translate Al Ghosaibi's *Dusting the Colour from Roses: Bilingual
Collection of Arabic Poetry*, published in 1995 by Saqi Books.

Abdul-Wahid Lu'Lu'Ah is a well-known scholar of Arabic poetry and
the translator of Kuwaiti poet Souad Al-Mubarak Al-Sabah's collection *In
the Beginning Was the Woman*.

Sarah Maguire is the founder and director of the Poetry Translation
Centre. She has published four collections of poetry: *Spilt Milk*, *The
Invisible Mender*, *The Florist's at Midnight*, and *The Pomegranates of Kandahar*.
With Sabry Hafez, she co-translated Mahmoud Darwish's *A State of Siege*.
With Yama Yari, she co-translated Atiq Rahimi's *A Thousand Rooms of Dream
and Fear*. Currently, she is working with Sabry Hafez to translate the work
of Al-Saddiq Al-Raddi.

Khaled Mattawa is originally from Benghazi, Libya. He is the author
of four books of poetry: *Tocqueville*, *Amorisco*, *Zodiac of Echoes*, and *Ismailia
Eclipse*. He has translated eight books of contemporary Arabic poetry
by Saadi Youssef, Fadhil Al-Azzawi, Hatif Janabi, Maram Al-Massri,
Joumana Haddad, Amjad Nasser, and Iman Mersal, and has co-edited two

anthologies of Arab-American literature. He has been awarded the PEN award for literary translation, a Guggenheim fellowship, the Alfred Hodder fellowship from Princeton University, a US National Endowment for the Arts Literary Translation Grant, and three Pushcart prizes. He is currently an associate professor in the Department of English at the University of Michigan.

Bahaa-eddin M. Mazid is an assistant professor in the Department of Translation Studies at United Arab Emirates University in Al Ain and Associate Professor of Linguistics and Translation at Sohag University, Egypt. His degrees include an MA in Teaching English as a Foreign Language and an MA and a PhD in Applied Linguistics. He has published extensively in both Arabic and English.

Fatima Mostafawi of Doha, Qatar is a 2008 graduate of Virginia Commonwealth University in Qatar, holding a BFA in Graphic Design. Her initial work on *Gathering the Tide* came under the auspices of an Undergraduate Research Experience Program grant awarded by the Qatar Foundation and the Qatar National Research Fund. She is currently Assistant Curator at the Arab Museum of Modern Art in Doha.

Anna Murison holds an MA in Arabic from the School of Oriental and African Studies, London, UK. She obtained her first degree in Arabic at the University of Edinburgh.

Ghassan Nasr received his BA from Indiana University, US and his MFA from the University of Arkansas. His translation of *The Journals of Sarab Affan: A Novel* by Jabra Ibrahim Jabra was published by Syracuse University Press in 2007. He is currently an assistant professor of English and Modern Languages at DePauw University, US.

Naomi Shihab Nye is the author of several books of poems, including *You and Yours* (BOA Editions 2005), which received the Isabella Gardner Poetry Award, as well as *19 Varieties of Gazelle: Poems of the Middle East* (2002), a collection of new and selected poems about the Middle East, *Fuel* (1998), *Red Suitcase* (1994), and *Hugging the Jukebox* (1982). She has been a Lannan Fellow, a Guggenheim Fellow, and a Wittner Bynne Fellow. In 1988, she received The Academy of American Poets' Lavan Award, selected by W. S. Merwin.

Wen Chin Ouyang is the author of *Literary Criticism in Medieval Islamic Culture: The Making of a Tradition*, and has contributed to many other works, including *Companion to Magical Realism* and *New Perspectives on the Arabian Nights: Ideological Variations and Narrative Horizons*. She lectures in Arabic Literature and Comparative Literature at the School of Oriental and African Studies, London.

The Poetry Translation Centre Workshop was established by UK poet Sarah Maguire (cf.) in 2004. The workshops pair poets and translators to translate contemporary poetry from Africa, Asia, and Latin America to a high literary standard.

Adrian Roscoe has held the chair of English in universities in Malawi, South Africa, and New Zealand and a visiting professorship in African and British literature at the State University of New York. He currently teaches at Sultan Qaboos University, Oman.

A. A. Ruffai collaborated with Heather Lawton and Saudi poet Ghazi Al Ghosaibi to translate Al Ghosaibi's *Dusting the Colour from Roses: Bilingual Collection of Arabic Poetry*, published in 1995 by Saqi Books.

Ayesha Saldanha was born in India, grew up in the UK, and lives in Bahrain, where she works as a translator, writer, and teacher.

Nehad Selaiha of Cairo holds a PhD in Drama from the School of Drama, University of Exeter, UK. She is the resident drama critic of the English-language newspaper *Al-Ahram Weekly* and is well known as a leading theater critic, writer, and translator. She has translated three collections of poetry by Kuwaiti poet Souad Al-Mubarak Al-Sabah as well as novels and plays by Mohamed Galal, Salah Abdel-Sabour, and Naguib Mahfouz.

Anton Shammas was born in northern Israel and studied English literature and art history at the Hebrew University of Jerusalem. Shammas is known primarily for his writing in Hebrew and Hebrew translations of Arab literature, such as the work of Emile Habibi. He is currently a professor of Middle Eastern literature at the University of Michigan, US.

Said M. Shiyab is chair of the Department of Translation Studies at United Arab Emirates University in Al Ain. He holds a PhD in Linguistics and Translation, Heriot-Watt University, Edinburgh, UK. With his areas of specialization including contrastive linguistics, translation and interpreting, sociolinguistics, pragmatics, systemic linguistics and discourse analysis, theories of applied linguistics, discourse and literary analysis, and translation studies, he has published widely in academic journals and publications.

Elizabeth Thomas is a widely published poet, performer, advocate of the arts, and teacher from the US. She is also the founder of UpWords Poetry, a company dedicated to promoting programs for young writers and educators.

Hart Uhl is a student of political science, English, and Arabic at Appalachian State University. This is his first translation work.

Nariman Youssef received her MS in Translation Studies from the University of Edinburgh, UK in 2008 and is now studying for a PhD at the University of Manchester, UK.

Abir Zaki has lived, worked, and studied in Paris, Beirut, Kabul, Istanbul, Mecca, Jeddah, and the US. She has a Master's degree in Education in Learning Difficulties from New York University, US and a Bachelor's degree in English Language and Literature from Jeddah University, Saudi Arabia. She published her first volume of poetry, *Poetic Aroma*, in 2004 and her second, *Wings of Freedom*, in 2008.

Joseph T. Zeidan received his BA in Arabic and English and his MA in Arabic from Hebrew University of Jerusalem and his PhD in Near Eastern Studies from the University of California, Berkeley. His Arabic-to-English literary translations include, with John Hinton, *Days of My Life* [Ayyam min Hayati] by Zeinab Al-Ghazali, *In Their Own Words: Testimonies of Arab Women Writers*, and poetry in *As the Words Turn Olive: Arab Women Poets in the Turning Century*, edited by Nathalie Handal. He is an associate professor of Arabic, Department of Near Eastern Languages and Cultures, at Ohio State University.

THE EDITORS

Patty Paine is the author of *The Sounding Machine* (Accents Publishing, 2012) and *Elegy & Collapse* (Finishing Line Press, 2005). Her poems, reviews, photographs, and interviews have appeared in *Gulf Stream*, *Blackbird*, *The Atlanta Review*, *The Southern Poetry Journal*, *Floorboard Review*, and numerous other journals. She is the founding editor of *diode poetry journal* and *diode editions*. Her scholarly work has appeared in *The International Journal of the Humanities*, *The Journal of the World Universities Forum*, and other journals. She is an assistant professor of English at Virginia Commonwealth University in Qatar, where she teaches writing and literature and is Assistant Director of Liberal Arts and Sciences.

Jeff Lodge is the author of the novel *Where This Lake Is* (White Pine Press, 1997). He has published fiction, poetry, and essays in *GSU Review*, *Makeout Creek*, *Persona*, *Pleiades*, *Squib*, and other publications and has written dozens of book reviews for the *Richmond Times-Dispatch* and *Style Weekly*, both of Richmond, Virginia, US. He is a founding and contributing editor of *Blackbird: an online journal of literature and the arts* and is co-editor of *diode poetry journal*. He is an assistant professor of core education at Virginia Commonwealth University in Richmond, Virginia.

Dr. Samia Touati is the author of *Literacy, Access to Information in Development in the Last Decade of the Twentieth Century Moroccan Society* (University Press of America, 2011). Her past research projects have included "Orality, Literacy and Secondary Orality: Rethinking Freshman Composition at an American University in 21st Century Qatar", linguistic diversity and the idea of the nation, and the sociolinguistic and semiotic study of speech variety in Morocco. A fluent speaker of English, French, and Arabic, she has translated several scholarly and academic projects, poems, formal/business letters, and biographies. She is an adjunct assistant professor of English at Virginia Commonwealth University in Qatar.

David Wojahn, author of the introduction, has published eight collections of poetry: *World Tree* (2011); *Interrogation Palace: New and Selected Poems*

1982–2004 (2006); *Spirit Cabinet* (2002); *The Falling Hour* (1997); *Late Empire* (1994); *Mystery Train* (1990); and *Glassworks* (1987, winner of the Society of Midland Authors Award), all from the University of Pittsburgh; and *Icehouse Lights* (1982, winner of the Yale Younger Poets Award). He is also the author of *Strange Good Fortune* (University of Arkansas, 2001), a collection of essays on contemporary verse. He is the editor (with Jack Myers) of *A Profile of Twentieth Century American Poetry* (1991). He also edited *The Only World* (1995), a posthumous collection of Lynda Hull's poetry. He has received fellowships from the John Simon Guggenheim Memorial Foundation, the National Endowment for the Arts, the Fine Arts Work Center in Provincetown, the Illinois Arts Council, the Indiana Arts Commission, and the Bread Loaf Writers' Conference, as well as writing residencies from the Yaddo and McDowell colonies. Among his other awards and honors are the Amy Lowell Poetry Traveling Scholarship; the William Carlos Williams Award and the Celia B. Wagner Award from the Poetry Society of America; Vermont College's Crowley/Weingarten Award for Excellence in Teaching; the George Kent Prize from *Poetry* magazine; and three Pushcart Prizes. His poetry, essays, and reviews have appeared in many journals and anthologies, among them *The Paris Review*, *The New Yorker*, *The Best American Poetry* series, *The American Poetry Review*, *The New York Times Book Review*, *The Chicago Tribune*, *The Kenyon Review*, *The New England Review*, *The Georgia Review*, and *TriQuarterly*. Wojahn teaches at Virginia Commonwealth University and in the low-residency MFA program at Vermont College. He lives in Richmond, Virginia.

CREDITS

The following works, listed in the order in which they appear, are reprinted with the kind permission of the poets, translators, and/or publishers. The scope of this work made it difficult at times, despite all efforts and intentions, to contact all translators and publishers. The editors regret any omissions. If you wish to contact the publisher, corrections will be made in subsequent editions.

"Body", "The Friends There", and "Poets" by Qassim Haddad, translated by Khaled Mattawa. *Banipal: Magazine of Modern Arab Literature*, Issue 3, Autumn/Winter 1998.

"Stone" and "Words from a Young Night" by Qassim Haddad, translated by Khaled Mattawa. *Blackbird: an online journal of literature and the arts*, Vol. 9 (No. 2), Fall 2010.

"From *Less Than Ink*" by Fawzia Al Sindi, translated by Bahaa-eddin M. Mazid, with Patty Paine. *Blackbird: an online journal of literature and the arts*, Vol. 9 (No. 2), Fall 2010.

"From *Psalm 23: To the Singer's Nectar*" by Ali Al Sharqawi, translated by Lena Jayyusi and Naomi Shihab Nye. *Modern Arabic Poetry*. Edited by Salma Khadra Jayyusi. Columbia University Press 1987.

"White Shame" by Adel Khozam, translated by Joseph T. Zeidan. *Blackbird: an online journal of literature and the arts*, Vol. 9 (No. 2), Fall 2010.

"Destiny" and "The Heroism of a Thread" by Adel Khozam, translated by Issa J. Boullata. *Banipal: Magazine of Modern Arab Literature*, Issue 30, Autumn/Winter 2007.

"Beyond Language" by Ali Al Sharqawi. *Pearl, Dreams of Shell: Anthology of Bahrain Contemporary Poetry*. Compiled and translated by Hameed Al Qaed. Publication of Shaikh Ebrahim Center for Culture and Research. US Publisher, Howling Dog Press 2007.

"Morning in Paris" by Ahmed ALajmi. *Pearl, Dreams of Shell: Anthology of Bahrain Contemporary Poetry*. Compiled and translated by Hameed Al Qaed. Publication of Shaikh Ebrahim Center for Culture and Research. US Publisher, Howling Dog Press 2007.

"In the Presence of the One I Love" and "No One" by Ali Abdulla Khalifa. *Pearl, Dreams of Shell: Anthology of Bahrain Contemporary Poetry.* Compiled and translated by Hameed Al Qaed. Publication of Shaikh Ebrahim Center for Culture and Research. US Publisher, Howling Dog Press 2007.

"Without Reason", "Couple", "Ray", and "Those Not For Me" by Hamda Khamis. *Pearl, Dreams of Shell: Anthology of Bahrain Contemporary Poetry.* Compiled and translated by Hameed Al Qaed. Publication of Shaikh Ebrahim Center for Culture and Research. US Publisher, Howling Dog Press 2007.

"Chief of Staff", "Missile", "Nights of War", "Pretext", "Soldier", "War Martyr", "War Poet", "War Reporter", and "War Traders" by Karim Radhi. *Pearl, Dreams of Shell: Anthology of Bahrain Contemporary Poetry.* Compiled and translated by Hameed Al Qaed. Publication of Shaikh Ebrahim Center for Culture and Research. US Publisher, Howling Dog Press 2007.

"A Woman from Kuwait" and "My Body is a Palm Tree that Grows on Bahr al-Arab" by Souad Al-Mubarak Al-Sabah, translated by Nehad Selaiha. *Fragments of a Woman.* Dar Sader Publishers, Beirut 1995.

"Female 2000" and "Ingratitude" by Souad Al-Mubarak Al-Sabah, translated by Abdul-Wahid Lu'Lu'Ah. *In the Beginning was the Woman.* Dar Sader Publishers, Beirut 1994.

"Love Poem 1" by Souad Al-Mubarak Al-Sabah, translated by Mohammed Ali Harfouch. *Love Poems.* Souad Al-Sabah Publishing House 2003.

"Escaping from the Coma Cage" and "The Sparkle" by Ghanima Zaid Al Harb. *The Echo of Kuwaiti Creativity: a Collection of Translated Kuwaiti Poetry.* Compiled and translated by Haifa Al Sanousi. Publication of Center for Research and Studies on Kuwait, 2006.

"The Harvest", "A Pulse", and "An Elegy" by Khalifa Al Woqayyan. *The Echo of Kuwaiti Creativity: a Collection of Translated Kuwaiti Poetry.* Compiled and translated by Haifa Al Sanousi. Publication of Center for Research and Studies on Kuwait, 2006.

"The Mural of Arrogance" by Mohammad Almoghrabi, translated by Khaled Al-Masri. *Blackbird: an online journal of literature and the arts,* Vol. 9 (No. 2), Fall 2010.

"Soon She Will Leave" by Saadia Mufarreh, translated by Hend Mubarek Aleidan, with Patty Paine. *Blackbird: an online journal of literature and the arts,* Vol. 9 (No. 2), Fall 2010.

"Speed" by Abudullah al Ryami, translated by the Poetry Translation Centre Workshop, with Anna Murison and "Please Don't Give Birth!"

by Abudullah al Ryami, translated by Sarah Maguire, with Nariman Youssef, Anna Murison, and Hafiz Kheir, Poetry Translation Centre. www.poetrytranslation.org.

"The Car" and "Malika and the Zar Dance" by Ghalya Al Said. *Blackbird: an online journal of literature and the arts*, Vol. 9 (No. 2), Fall 2010.

"A Little Before Reaching Death" and "Apology to the Dawn" by Mohamed al-Harthy, translated by Camilo Gómez-Rivas. *Banipal: Magazine of Modern Arab Literature*, Issue 20, Summer 2004.

"Pawns of Sand" and "At a Slant Angle" by Mohamed al-Harthy, translated by Sargon Boulus. *Banipal: Magazine of Modern Arab Literature*, Issue 4, Spring 1999.

"May Love Be Praised" by Reem Al Lawati, translated by Issa J. Boullata. *Blackbird: an online journal of literature and the arts*, Vol. 9 (No. 2), Fall 2010.

"The Flood" by Soad Al Kuwari, translated by Fatima Mostafawi, with Patty Paine and "Modernity in the Desert" by Soad Al Kuwari, translated by Sara Al Qatami, with Patty Paine. *Blackbird: an online journal of literature and the arts*, Vol. 9 (No. 2), Fall 2010.

"Emergency Meeting" by Abdullah Al Salem, translated by William M. Hutchins. *Blackbird: an online journal of literature and the arts*, Vol. 9 (No. 2), Fall 2010.

"Arrival", "Distant Waters", "Museum of Shadows", "No Country We Headed To", "Under the Roofs of Morning", and "Water Blessed by Prophets", "Scream", and "A Tramp Dreaming of Nothing" by Saif Al Rahbi, translated by Anton Shammas. *Banipal: Magazine of Modern Arab Literature*, Issue 23, Summer 2005.

"The Angel of Power", "A Room at the End of the World", and "Those Years" by Zahir Al Ghafri, translated by Salih J. Altoma. *Banipal: Magazine of Modern Arab Literature*, Issue 19, Spring 2004.

"Little Tales", from *Journals of the Self* by Zakiyya Malallah, translated by Wen Chin Ouyang. *The Poetry of Arab Women: A Contemporary Anthology*. Edited by Nathalie Handal. Interlink Publishing Group, 2000.

"Illusions and Realities" and "Freedom Writers" by Nimah Ismail Nawwab. *Blackbird: an online journal of literature and the arts*, Vol. 9 (No. 2), Fall 2010.

"The Signs" by Ali Al Domaini, translated by Laith al-Husain and Patricia Alanah Byrne. *Beyond the Dunes: An Anthology of Modern Saudi Literature*. Edited by Mansour al-Hazimi, Ezzat Khattab, and Salma Khadra Jayyusi. I. B. Tauris, 2006.

"Gray Hair" by Ashjan Al Hendi, translated by Abdulla Al-Harrasi, with Adrian Roscoe. *Blackbird: an online journal of literature and the arts*, Vol. 9 (No. 2), Fall 2010.

"Moon Wars" by Ashjan Al Hendi, translated by Laith al-Husain, with Alan Brownjohn. *Beyond the Dunes: An Anthology of Modern Saudi Literature.* Edited by Mansour al-Hazimi, Ezzat Khattab, and Salma Khadra Jayyusi. I. B. Tauris, 2006.

"Numerical Conjecture" by Fowziyah Abu-Khalid, translated by Ghassan Nasr, with Joseph Heithaus. *Blackbird: an online journal of literature and the arts*, Vol. 9 (No. 2), Fall 2010.

"Tuful: Noonday Rainbow" by Fowziyah Abu-Khalid, translated by Ruanne Abou-Rahme and Patricia Alanah Byrne, and "Two Little Girls" by Fowziyah Abu-Khalid, translated by Jinan M. Coulter and Patricia Alanah Byrne. *Beyond the Dunes: An Anthology of Modern Saudi Literature.* Edited by Mansour al-Hazimi, Ezzat Khattab, and Salma Khadra Jayyusi. I. B. Tauris, 2006.

"The Poet" and "Sword" by Abdallah Al Saikhan, translated by Ayesha Saldhana. *Blackbird: an online journal of literature and the arts*, Vol. 9 (No. 2), Fall 2010.

"Immigrant" by Nujoom Alghanem, translated by Khaled Mattawa. *Blackbird: an online journal of literature and the arts*, Vol. 9 (No. 2), Fall 2010.

"A mad man who does not love me" by Maisoon Saqr Al Qasimi, translated by Khaled Mattawa. *Banipal: Magazine of Modern Arab Literature*, Issue 17, Summer 2003.

"All That We Have" by Khalid Albudoor. *Blackbird: an online journal of literature and the arts*, Vol. 9 (No. 2), Fall 2010.